# The Inner Journey of Energy and Spirit

## Blended Theory of Psychology and Mindfulness

I0156783

Gregory Rubin

ISBN-10: 0692325298
ISBN-13: 978-0692325292

# Gratitude

There are people whom I keep very close to my heart that I would like to acknowledge. People who have helped me tremendously along the way in all categories of my life; supporting me, loving me, teaching me, and allowing me to be a part of their world. In accordance with how I live, how I love, and how I work, it is vital to the momentum of this book for me to be able to start with positive energy coming directly from my heart. I want to share my appreciation in this forum, yet I also want to be mindful about privacy and not excluding anyone.

I am a firm believer, regardless of our age, circumstances, wisdom, or success, that we are in a constant state of learning and growth. For that reason, I am profoundly grateful for the opportunity to know and work with so many people who have helped me to formulate the ideas and philosophies that I live by and work by. Every single person that I have met in my office has contributed to teaching me more about people, life, love, simplicity, and even in my own self-identity. I have written a special "thank you" that remains in my office waiting room. I would like to share it briefly here:

"To all of those reading this, I wish to express my deepest appreciation for your confidence and trust. I wish to honor your courage and determination and I thank you from the bottom of my heart. May your journey be filled with peace and joy".

To the special people in my life, I am asking that you search your hearts and souls. If I have done a good enough job of practicing what I preach, then you already know how much you mean to me. You know that I cherish you, no matter what your role is in my life, and you know that I give all that I can because you are worth it to me and because you have earned a special place in my heart. I also wish to mention that there are some people who have done so much to love and support me, that I literally could not have traveled my path without them. They know who they are because they have been with me every step of the way from the very beginning. They have helped to formulate the idea of turning a passion and desire to help others into a career path that supports my family. They have created the guidance, supervision, office space, and confidence to pursue my ideas and to free my mind from the parameters of tradition and conventional thought; thus helping me to establish my own path and to follow my intuition. It is with great honor that I thank the two most responsible for helping me to drop the career pebble in the pond to start the ripple waves. I spend a lot of time honoring them in my heart and in my daily work, feeling appreciation for the humble start they gave me.

Then there is one person who has allowed me to share a life with her; one who has given me true meaning and purpose and who has provided me with the love that I needed to feel valuable and worthy of goodness. She has created a family for us, a home, and has somehow found a way to nurture us each step of the way. The fact that she lets me love her amazes me to this day. She makes me want to be a better person and she is the source of so much of what I do and why I do it. Thank you, Madeline, for being my best friend, my partner, my wife, and the mother of our wonderful children.

# Contents

# Introduction

After sitting with people in their darkest moments and their happiest moments for the past 15 years, I have seen remarkable resiliency in the face of devastation and amazing examples of life changing moments. It remains a humbling honor for me to be invited into people's worlds, to be trusted with such sensitive/intense information, and to aide in guiding people to making changes that allow them the joy and peace that they deserve. Much of my limited expertise has come from personal trial and error, as well as gaining experience from learning about what works and does not work in other people's lives.

I have noticed that there are patterns that affect all of us, no one is immune to pain and suffering or trials and tribulations. There seem to be waves of negativity and extreme stress, sometimes attributed to holidays, seasonal/climate changes, the moon and stars, or even political/societal movements. When things come together, it is as if I see how the universe works with all of my senses. I believe that if we tap into this correctly, if we follow the signs and signals in front of us, we can navigate through the rapids, getting across safely to our destination. Sometimes this can be done with a strong mindfulness and intention, and other times, it can be done through other people or other forces looking out for us-protecting us and creating pathways for us to follow.

It is my most sincere desire that this book offers the beginning steps of a new way of thinking, feeling, behaving, sensing, and experiencing of yourself and the world around you. It is not a "how to" or "instructional manual," it is merely a template to foster creative thinking and using other senses beyond what you think of as logic and reason to help you make decisions and help in your perception of experiences. I have become such a believer in these concepts that I am accustomed to operating in extreme and counter-intuitive ways. It is for this reason why I think that many people may not understand "why" I do things or "what" guides me to make certain decisions. I can appreciate and respect how hard it will be to utilize new guiding principles in your life.

I am suggesting that you take your time, pace yourself, and find ways to take these macro-level approaches to funnel down to a micro-level way of operating. Start with something simple, something that allows you the ability to operate somewhat out of your comfort zone. However, start at a pace that does not cause you new/further distress. If we look at a martial arts philosophy/mentality for a moment, let us consider the analogy of a black belt. In much of our western culture, we believe that to be of the highest rank, status, and skill. Yet, it is a widely held belief that earning a black belt in martial arts signifies the beginning of the student's training. It represents having demonstrated the basic knowledge required to build upon the skills needed to live the philosophy. Looking at energy theory in that way, we should strive for higher enlightenment and a sense of a life long journey, not simply steps taken to get to the next level.

Consider for a moment the confidence that financial security brings, or the trust in a GPS device to navigate a destination, or the sense of security in developing martial arts skills. Think about how much of existence is unknown, ambiguous, and out of a person's control. What if there were a way to ground yourself in every aspect of your life? A way that can offer you the ability to follow the signals and data presented in front of you to make decisions, to solve problems, and to manifest an abundance of positive energy within and around you? The energy theory suggested in this book is my attempt to illustrate an example of how to anchor yourself in the midst of an emotional tornado that is out of control and is potentially life threatening. In the following pages, it is my hope that you will build upon a network of ideas and principles that will create enough emotional stability and energy balance to provide you with the tools to solve any obstacle in front of you. This book can serve as a guide to share a philosophy that goes beyond the basic principles of faith, or having a positive outlook, and seeing life as a glass half full. To me, these are wonderful tools available to us, but they do not necessarily offer a template for finding specific answers to specifics problems.

As you read through this book, it is important to keep in mind that the true essence of this energy theory rests within your mind, body, and spirit. And, please keep in mind that no one can be told how to live their life or how to operate within energy theory. It requires a philosophical shift and metamorphosis that taps into your own inner creative ability and mixes with a strong spiritual energy source that surrounds you. You may notice having a reaction to the word "spiritual" or "spirituality." It is important to pay attention to any reaction and to be mindful of how you want to experience and perceive this book and its intentions. For the sake of clarity, the term "spirituality" is used specifically in this book as a term that encompasses a wide range of philosophical beliefs, scientific/mathematical principles, sociological themes, and religious views. Think of it as a holistic blending of your six senses (sight, smell, taste, touch, hearing, and intuition) to make sense out of the sensory input and data that is around you in a sacred way.

There are many principles, philosophies, and religious teachings/scripture that I believe encompass the essence of energy theory: Here are a few: The golden rule-treat others as you would want to be treated; focus on helping things to go right-rather than trying to prevent things from going wrong; one often meets his destiny on the road he takes to avoid it; and from scripture; *yea, though I walk through the valley of the shadow of death, I will fear no evil, for thou art with me, thy rod and thy staff they comfort me.*

If we consider components of Asian culture/eastern philosophy, we can look at the fundamental principle of Kung Fu. "Kung Fu is in everything that we do, how we put on a jacket, how we take off a jacket, how we treat people, and how we live." Energy theory suggests the same connection between how we choose to live our lives and what we get from the world around us as a result. It is more than just Karma or asking the question, "What would Jesus do?" Energy theory explores the interdependence that exists between each of us as individuals and the positive and negative spirit that surrounds us each day. It is about tapping into energy sources around us to help navigate and guide us through every minute of our existence. It is a principle based GPS system that can provide turn-by-turn directions in decision making and managing emotions. Because so much of our existence rests in ambiguity (the unknown), we can easily get lost, confused, overwhelmed, and short-circuited by all of the input data around us; sensory overload.

Energy theory encompasses a blend of the creative/artistic life force inside of us (divine energy) and a methodological and logical diagnostic operating system. We can nurture our ability to do these things and train ourselves, like a black belt martial artist, to harness this energy into great internal power and control. Yet, with this skill comes an extreme responsibility to find balance and harmony within ourselves and within the people and environment that surround us. It incorporates a Native American philosophy of living in unison with nature, taking only what we need and giving back enough to replenish our resources. Think of living in complete harmony with every aspect of the symphony of life; every individual note being pure and vital to the entire piece, yet not over taking the beauty of the holistic experience of the symphony. In the movie Avatar, it was said that *there is a network of energy that flows through all living things, and, all energy is only borrowed and one day you have to give it back.* The giving back of energy can be viewed in many different ways, but it reminds me about a concept that I learned from the people I have worked with in substance abuse recovery- "you have to give it away to keep it"-namely, your sobriety, your positive energy/life force, the karma that you build in this life, etc. In order to keep something, you have to be willing and able to send it back out into the universe.

# *Chapter 1*

# Dilemmas

To further investigate how energy theory explores the interdependence that exists between each of us as individuals and the positive and negative spirit that surrounds us each day, we can start to look at some practical dilemmas that we may find ourselves in. The following is the beginning baseline for how to be mindful about energy theory and how to apply it for every day use.

In a scenario in which a person is looking for a job based on financial necessity or based on a career change, let us map out things that people would typically consider. The first would be the basic job description, asking yourself if this job is within your area of expertise or training. Is this a job that you could see yourself doing? What is the salary/pay, the health-care benefits, the commute, etc.? These are all valid things to be mindful of during this job search. Yet, there are risks and pitfalls that can block the "energy flow" and can ultimately lead you to accept a job that may not be a good fit, or to decline a job that could enhance and nurture you in unexpected ways.

Based on energy theory concepts, it is important to expand the scope of what we pay attention to and what we allow to influence us during this process. For example, money can be one of the biggest barriers and blocks to following energy theory correctly. We typically have a love/hate relationship with money: we recognize the importance of it, yet also disdain the power that it has over us, society, etc. Money is not the root of all evil, but it can create what I call a "short circuit" where it disrupts our ability to find anchoring to make decisions. Notice the symbolic irony in the fact that we existentially know that money should not be our God, yet we print "In God We Trust" directly on our money. Is that a mixed message? Or, perhaps it is an anchoring reminder that it is God to trust, not the power/influence money can have? I will discuss this dichotomy I call "meta-messages" (the message within the message-the notion of what we are actually communicating) later in this book.

Back to the issue of money, money is certainly a very important factor in the decision to pursue and accept a job, yet it can also be our downfall. One of the worst jobs I ever had was a job in which I submitted my two week resignation letter after only two weeks of working there. This job voluntarily offered me $5k more in salary than I expected and asked for. I did not stop to ask myself, why they were offering me this "extra" money. The concern about money is valid and it should factor into a job decision to some extent. However, if we can remove the here-and-now concern regarding money, it can be a freeing agent to help us more creatively work on this decision. Consider the emotional and physical costs of a person who works strictly for the paycheck and dreads Sundays because they are one day closer to his/her work week starting again. Do you know of someone in that category? Or is it you? What about the mentality of "life is tough kid, nothing is fair, you get a job, it sucks, and that's how the world works?" What message does that send about accepting negative things in our lives? On the opposite end of the spectrum, imagine a job that was internally fulfilling, a job that allowed you to operate within your skill sets and interests. What if that job offered you $5k less per year? Would it be worth it? It is hard to put a financial number on a concept that is ambiguous but extremely important.

With that said, here are some other things to consider using energy theory as a guiding principle in this job search example. What were the circumstances in which you came across this job opportunity? Was it through a networking opportunity, or during a random search online, did you call directly to inquire about employment, did they seek you out, etc? Also, consider why you are applying for the job, are you trying to extract yourself from a current toxic situation, is the commute wearing on you, are you trying to jump-start your career or are you trying to wind-down in your career?

While these things begin to marinate in the back of your mind, start to pay attention to other important signs and signals. Things like, how did I feel when I first learned about this job, who was I with, what was I thinking/doing just before I found out about it? If you had an opportunity to speak with someone on the phone before you are offered an interview, how did they sound, what did they say, is there anything that stood out as significant to you about the person and/or the organization in which he/she represents? If you are asked to come in for an interview, pay attention to everything! Pay attention to the ride along the way to the destination (was it pleasant or unpleasant, does it remind you of anything), the layout of the parking lot, the building, the reception area, the colors, the décor, flourescent lighting, etc. And during the interview, try to think of it as you interviewing them as well, is this a place that you want to spend between 8-10 hours per day for 5 days in a row?

Pay attention to all of your sensory inputs and what may be broadcast to you on an energy level. These things are critical as you collect your data to later determine anchor points in making a decision. You are at risk by allowing money, a current toxic situation, or any external pressure to influence your decisions; things like "in this economy, it would be foolish to turn down any job." Having this mentality will likely defeat you before you even get started. Using this first dilemma as an example, we can see some of the common short circuits impeding a person's ability to make an informed decision about accepting a job, or even what jobs to apply for.

*Chapter 2*

# Meta-Messages

Before I write some more in-depth examples about utilizing energy theory. I want to take a detour into the realm of meta-messages. A meta-message can be defined as what is actually being communicated at a higher level beyond the content of what is being said. It can be described as "the message within the message" or perhaps "reading in between the lines." We communicate at multiple levels at once, utilizing all of our senses to help us interpret and make sense out of the data that we are receiving. It is my belief that most of what we respond and react to are from the meta messages received by others. These messages are sometimes subtle and sometimes overt, yet we process them in milliseconds and often in subconscious or emotionally reactive ways.

For example, we all have had frustrating brief experiences with strangers that have left a bad taste in our mouth; whether that was a customer service interaction, someone passing by in a store/place of business, in the elevator, holding the door open for someone, on the road, etc. Most of us seem to be very good at recognizing meta-messages on a subconscious level, but not very good at the mindfulness about them and how to respond in a "situation matching" type of way. Mindfulness can be defined as maintaining awareness of our thoughts, feelings, sensations, and surrounding environment. Mindfulness involves examination with clear intent, objectivity, and without judgment or valuation. I define "situation matching" as a response pattern that is appropriate and matching to a person's meta-message he/she delivered. It could be in a moment of compassion, for example, a friend of yours who loses a loved one and breaks down during a movie you are watching together; "I just can't do this without [loved one] anymore." The meta-message being sent is "he/she was very important to me, my life is forever changed and I don't know how to adjust to this change." The appropriate response to your friend would be "I know you love [person] so much, he/she was so important to you and it's tough to know how to endure this loss and pain." The meta-message that you are sending back is "I am here for you, I care about you, and you are not alone and will not have to go through this by yourself."

Another situation matching type of meta-message can be in the realm of deflecting negative energy or de-escalating a situation. I would like to add a disclaimer that there is not a one size fits all type of approach. You have to find an approach that works for you, that allows you to respond in a way that is consistent with who you are, and in a way that does not further complicate situations or create negative energy that you could feel guilt/remorse about. For example, I was asked one time from a business solicitor if I wanted to earn a free dinner to a local restaurant by giving my personal information for a mailer and listening to a brief presentation about the products that he was selling. This occurred during a family trip to a local fair. Being that I very much cherish the limited time that I get with my family, I was interested in enjoying the moment and was not interested in consuming more products or services (i.e., I did not need to buy a fence or new tile for my bathroom). The interaction went as follows with the meta-messages included in parenthesis.

Solicitor: "Hi, would you like to earn a free dinner tonight?" (meta-message- I have something that I want to sell you and I will use marketing tactics to draw you in).

Me: "Thank you for the offer but I'll pass, no thank you." (meta-message- Please leave me alone, I know that you have a job to do but maybe you can move onto the next person).

Solicitor: "Why not, don't you like to go out to dinner, especially for free?"

(meta-message- I will not accept no for an answer, I will bait you into a conversation that corners you into doing what I want you to do, and I will do so by asking you a ridiculous question that suggests that something is wrong with you if you do not comply).

Me: "No, I don't like to go out to dinner, especially for free." (meta-message- I will not be bullied or manipulated, I will give you a ridiculous answer to your ridiculous question and hopefully that will disarm you so you will move onto your next target). On a side note, this was said with no anger/frustration, no sarcasm, just neutrality.

Solicitor: "Why not, everyone likes to go out to dinner?" (meta-message- I do not accept your answer and I will continue to portray a picture that something must really be wrong with you if you do not answer my question correctly. I am up for the challenge of cornering you into hearing what I have to say about the product that I am selling).

Before I mention my final response, I want to share my inner thoughts and philosophy. At this point in time, I was still walking past his table, trying to be polite, being mindful of the meta communication occurring from both of us. I was intrigued by his aggressive tactics and I felt that it paralleled bullying, and from a community service standpoint, I felt a responsibility to try to help this guy to understand that this is not the way to do business and not the way to treat people. I was not upset with him, I was aware that it was his job and livelihood and that he was trained in this manner. It seemed like an energy short circuit to me. I was also a tad surprised that my first attempt to disarm him did not work, thinking that he would have be taken back by my response that I did not like to go out to dinner. I see now that it likely provoked him because I was matter of fact about my response. I have asked a hundred people or so how they would have handled the situation and the answers ranged from: "I would have said no, ignored the rest and walked away," "I would have said no, please leave me alone, or I that I may come back later if I change my mind," and many people admitted that they would have likely stood there engaged in the conversation, feeling trapped and not wanting to be "rude." Two extremes would have been to allow yourself to be controlled by the solicitor, or to allow yourself to get angry/frustrated and short or snappy.

In the split second before my final response, I remember thinking to myself that I was going to have to not only disarm him more effectively, but that I wanted him to think twice about how he is engaging people. I knew that if I was direct he <u>may</u> stop, but that he would not likely think twice about the interaction. He could easily ignore my sentiment and move onto the next "victim." I thought that I needed to deliver my message swiftly and without anger and that I needed this interaction to linger within him. So, as he asked me the final question about why I did not like to go out to dinner because "everyone likes to go out to dinner," here is what came out of my mouth when I stopped, paused, looked him in the eyes and peacefully said:

"Well, actually sir (pause…….), it's against my religion to go out to dinner." (meta-message- I am going to execute my finishing move as if this where a martial arts tournament and I will tell you something that is extremely controversial, religion, to try to get you to understand that you cannot plow over people in disregard for them without there being some form of consequence to them or you. I will use guilt in this example to let you know that you have crossed several lines and need to rethink your methods).

While I am not condoning being dishonest or utilizing religion in any disrespectful way; it is my belief that we have to occasionally utilize outside of the box methods to extract ourselves out of negative situations or for problem solving. To me, this is similar to a flexibility in what we typically deem as black or white ways of operating. As an example, is it wrong to drive over the posted speed limit? Many will say "yes, it's against the law."

Yet, we do not really have enough information to answer that question, what if we are driving to the emergency room? According to our legal system, it is still considered unlawful and unjustified, yet I am willing to accept that and take the risk, in this example, because it means getting a loved one the medical treatment that they need.

In the free dinner scenario example, the solicitor quickly responded with a sincere apology and further went on to say that he hoped that my family and I had a nice rest of our evening. He was shocked at my response and seemed to understand that he crossed a line. That was my goal and what I said to him was effective. I did not want to be mean but I was thinking about a martial arts mentality. A trained person of martial arts will understand that his/her skills are not to be utilized for fighting, but often for conflict avoidance and for peaceful interactions. A trained professional in martial arts will have a confidence that he/she can defend him/herself, yet will be extremely cautious about using his/her highly trained skills. In the event that a conflict is unavoidable, the martial artist is trained to do what is needed to de-escalate the threat, to stop the attacker, and to leave the situation as quickly as possible. It is not typically within the training or mentality to then make the person "pay for" attacking him/her by using martial arts skills any further.

The interaction with the solicitor represents an energy short circuit within him that illustrates this inner reality:

> I need to do this job to make money to support myself or my family, I will not allow anyone or anything to get in my way of making the money that I need. I am willing to do whatever it takes and I have been trained to ignore and dismiss your feelings so that I can profit from my ability to catch you off guard enough to pull you into what I need you to do.

My situation matching solution was to respond with:

> I accept your need and desire to support yourself and your family, I honor that, yet I will not allow myself to be bullied, manipulated, or blamed for your profit. I will attempt to resolve this peacefully, but if you continue to back me into a corner, I will have to respond in a way that stops you in your tracks and makes you rethinking what you are doing.

## Chapter 3

# The Message of the Chair

The chair scenario energy principle represents a short circuit that occurs frequently for my co-workers and clients when I worked for a short time as a psychotherapist in a community mental health center. To give a brief background, I had been working as a psychotherapist in part-time private practice for about 2 years while I was finishing my graduate studies. I accepted a full time job at a prestigious local hospital in their adult outpatient mental health program shortly after earning my Master's degree. We were a satellite office located about a mile from the main hospital campus and we worked with people who suffered from chronic mental illness, substance use, and some with criminal backgrounds. Many of the people we served were not able to work, function well in society, or maintain interpersonal relationships.

My mindset as a psychotherapist has always been that of having extreme respect for the people that I work with and a genuine care for them as humans with unique experiences. I believe in working in a collaborative way and learning from each other along the way. One of the things that I have always believed in was the importance of the physical environment in any helping profession. I believe that it can set the stage for the therapeutic relationship to form, for the healing that is intended to take place, and for creating a nurturing environment to foster growth and critical thought. This environment should convey professionalism, respect for the guests that come there, and having décor that reflects the nature of the helping profession.

With that said, my first office was an 8x8 square foot space in the back corner of the facility, not much larger than a broom closet. After several months, I had an opportunity to move my office closer to the rest of my colleagues near the main entrance and reception area. This new 9x9 square foot office was certainly an upgrade for me at the time. I spent an entire weekend "after hours" painting the walls, re-arranging the sparse furniture, adding decorations, and bringing in the "chair." The "chair" was a black leather recliner purchased from Wal-Mart for $199. I was excited to bring this chair to the office because I thought it would add to the experience of relaxation, comfort, healing, and safety that I wanted to create for my clients.

After several hours of working on my new office space, attending to every square inch of the 9x9 office with the thought of comfort and safety for my clients, I marveled in my small accomplishment. A transformation of a fluorescent light "cube" into a cozy therapeutic office. As Monday morning approached, I eagerly looked forward to seeing my first clients in that space. I had arrived earlier than usual that day to get acclimated to my new environment. As each of my colleagues trickled into work that morning, I noticed some very surprising reactions from them. They were all excited to see the work that I had done and gave me good feedback about the decisions that I made. Yet, the "chair" quickly became the focal point as they made comments about my own comfort throughout the day and what it will feel like to conduct therapy from that type of chair (or to take naps in it during the day and some joked). I was very puzzled because I thought it was clear that this chair was strictly for my clients and not for my own use.

Given the layout of my office, its small size, and the fact that the only other chair in the room was a small swivel chair that sat in front of my desk facing the back wall, I thought it was obvious that this special leather chair was for clients and guests to sit in. I felt a moment of anxiety and doubt that perhaps I did not achieve optimal placement of the furniture and that the flow in the room was not as intuitive as I thought. During the next 30 minutes as the rest of my colleagues continue to arrive at work, I noticed very consistent reactions from them (about 8-9 people in total). As the pattern continued, I felt a sadness as I realized how far my perspective in this profession was from mainstream. My self-doubt dissipated quickly, despite my newness to the profession. I asked myself, how could this be? Why did my colleagues, with all of those combined years of experience, react so consistently? What did this mean? What did it say about our profession and our perspectives? Either way, to me this represented a need for a major shift in our work.

I reminded myself of the positive intent to create a nurturing environment for my clients and I decided that I was on the right track. I merely needed to trust my intuition that this new office would allow me to travel further into the individual worlds of my clients. The sadness grew in me as I felt a loss for people who seek counseling; a subtle loss of the respect for their humanity and for their experiences to be our main focus for the entire time that they are in our office. In the first two weeks that followed my office change, I was able to see all of the people in my caseload, and I paid very close attention to their reactions and changes in the nature of our work together. Sadly, the reactions from my clients were consistent with my colleagues.

Most of my clients actually walked into the office for the first time, passed the chair, stood in the center of the room, and asked where they should sit. They seemed to enjoy the office at first, looking at the pictures and decorations, but then had a genuine confusion about where their place was in the office. Each and every time I mentioned that the chair they walked by was theirs to sit in, they had a mixed looked on their face of surprise and confusion. They would say "wow, I get to sit in this chair, I must be somebody important," to which I replied "you are most certainly important and I want you to feel that every time you come here." While I was happy to create the space for them to feel respected and nurtured, it remained sad to me that they were reacting to this gesture as if it was the first time they were treated this way in their lives. For most of them, it truly was the first time in which they were genuinely respected. Many of them came from poverty, from drug/alcoholic homes, and they were labeled chronically mentally ill. By the end of the second week, as I was still introducing clients to the office, some came in and said right away "I couldn't wait to get here, I heard about the chair." (from other clients)

Another powerful moment came as I walked to the waiting room to greet the last person in my caseload to visit my office. She was a woman who had lost her eyesight several years before she and I met. She took my arm as we walked down the hallway to my office because I mentioned that we had a new route to walk due to my relocation. I can still hear the tapping of her walking cane as she struggled to enter the new doorway. She found the chair with her cane and she stopped right in her tracks. It did not make a solid tap sound, instead, it was muffled thud from the leather and cushion. She was very alarmed, not wanting to make a false move. I stopped with her for a moment and allowed her time to absorb the data she was collecting. She said, "what did I just hit?" I said, "it is your chair to sit in when you are here." She paused for another moment and said "it was quiet, does that mean it's leather?" I said, "Well the tag said it was leather but I'm not sure if it is real leather." She smiled and found her way to sit down. She was quite for a moment and asked if I had scented candles in the room. I did have candles in the room, they were fresh out of the box and were not lit. She continued to smile and said "I have never been treated like this before, most people ignore me because I'm blind." Her smile faded away and I gave her a moment to herself before I replied with "that makes me sad to hear that, but you do not have to feel 'less than' when you are here."

The "chair" served as a very symbolic anchor point for me early in my career. Not only did it give me a harsh lesson within the mainstream dynamics of therapy and the relationships between the therapist and client, but it seemed to unlock so much therapeutic content that we would never have had the opportunity to reveal without this catalyst. In the weeks following this profound discovery, clients and co-workers continued to make comments about the office and the chair. It served as a positive thing for my clients but perhaps as somewhat of an irritant for some of my co-workers. I believe that it stood out in an uncomfortable way for them, subtly challenging how they conduct their own therapeutic practice-whispering in their ear that there was a call to change. Though it was never my intent for that to happen, I am proud that it seemed to stir something in our group office.

The legacy of the chair continued even 6-8 months later as our small satellite office was moved to the main campus of the hospital. Interestingly enough, as we joined the "main group" in the adult outpatient psychiatric program, we all quickly felt the not so subtle message that there was a hierarchy in place and a collective consciousness that we were not allowed to penetrate. Our presence was unsettling to the main crew that had already established themselves there and they made it very clear that we were not welcome. Being the new kid on the block, I was relegated to another back office. "No problem" I thought to myself, "I can recreate what I just did only several months before." There was a resurgence of activity about the chair and, in the first few weeks, I had several unknown visitors walking by my office. People would pop their head in and say "Oh, you're the guy with the chair. I heard about you and wanted to see for myself." I soon discovered that these pop-ins were not compliments to me and my decorating; they were check-ins by my new colleagues to see if I was receiving things that they were not. I was asked very directly on several occasions "did _____(hospital) give you this chair, who gave it to you, where did you get it," etc. After I told them that I brought it in myself, on my own time and dime, they asked me with disdain in their eyes "why would you do that, that doesn't make any sense?" I would mostly shrug my shoulders and replied, "Well, I'm new to this and haven't learned all the rules around here. Thanks for stopping by." On a side note, I received my final pop in about three months after our move to the main campus. I asked that person who she was and she mentioned that she was from the other side of the campus, but that people were still talking about the "guy with the chair."

As an end to the chair story, I would like to share something that occurred regarding the chair on my last day of work at the hospital. I was moving my personal belongings to my vehicle and had just the chair and a couple of picture frames left. I decided to move the chair next and began the long walk (at least 600ft) down the hallway, two flights of stairs, and to my vehicle in the parking lot. Thank goodness I moved furniture as a job during college. I came back for the last of the picture frames, said some brief goodbyes, and made my way back to the parking lot from my office for the last time. When I got to my vehicle, I found a security team of two campus security guards peering into the vehicle at my possessions. In an instant, I felt a soothing sense of humor in the cosmic justice of things traveling full circle......the beginning of this job was not exactly smooth and it is fitting the ending it would not be very smooth either. I asked if I could help them with anything and they mentioned that they received a phone call from someone reporting that an employee was removing furniture/property from the building.

Ah yes, "the chair," controversy again. They promptly asked me if I was removing furniture from the property. Since I was in an appreciative mood that the chair had created turmoil for others yet again, those whom I fundamentally disagreed with their professional philosophies, I wanted to be patient and to see where this road would take us. I replied with "yes, I did take this chair from my office and intend on removing it from the property." They said, "Oh, so this was an accurate report that someone was removing furniture from the property." Still feeling patient and in control, I mention that the report was accurate but that I was extremely confused as to why two security guards were concerned with my personal belongings.

They asked if I knew that it was illegal to take things from the hospital's property, and I replied with "I most certainly understand that it would be illegal if I were stealing, but I am confused that we are having a conversation about me taking my own property, including this chair, home with me on my last day of work." They looked confused and clarified that I was the owner of the chair, a question that they had not considered asking in the beginning. I confirmed that I was the owner and had simply wished to go upstairs to get my last picture from my office. They left, still looking confused and told me to have a nice day. In all sincerity I can tell you that one of the security officers said that it was a "nice chair" just before he closed to door to his vehicle. And on that note, I left the hospital on my terms, feeling justified in the importance and the power of the chair.

## Chapter 4

# Intention and Mindfulness

The story of the impact the mere presence of the chair had on my clients and colleagues exemplifies one of my guiding beliefs; intention and mindfulness can influence and alter the course of events, circumstances, and people's perceptions. I also found it fascinating that a physical item had the ability to illicit so much from those in its vicinity. Perhaps the intention and vision of what I wanted to create in the office environment for my clients was channeled from a metaphysical/spiritual realm directly into our physical reality? I wonder if people could almost hear the whisper of my intention in their ears upon glancing at the chair.

In the next example, I will outline a scenario in which a peer in a graduate school class felt very strongly that she operated in a clear and fair way regarding intention and mindfulness. Using this example, I hope to illustration that intention and mindfulness are not the only things that factor into our ability to see the bigger picture and to attend to the energy and direction that we are signaled to follow.

This was a class in multicultural awareness and sensitivity. We were told to separate in small groups and to discuss a personal example of either a success in the area of expressing multicultural sensitivity, or an example of a failure to do so. Being the very eager and astute graduate students we were (sarcasm), we all naturally gravitated towards sharing a success rather than a failure. I suspect at this stage of my career and at my current level of self-awareness and humility, I would choose differently today. We each went through describing a brief scenario which seemingly showcased our social awareness and evolution; at least in each speaker's opinion. Interestingly enough, I was caught off guard by one student's comments about her success in that area. Upon first glance, it would appear that she had accurately made a good and fair decision based on the data she had available to her. Yet, there was something that existentially and energetically bothered me about her scenario; it illustrated the paradox that can occur when someone tries so hard to prevent something that it can actually contribute to creating the very thing that they are trying to prevent.

This woman was a hiring manager for a very large, well-known, and successful communications business. She always came to our evening classes directly from her full time job and was professional, polite, energetic, and obviously courageous in her pursuits to further her education and career. I found her to be pleasant and she seemed to have some valuable knowledge and wisdom to offer us in classroom discussions.

During this exercise, she discussed a scenario in which she was in charge of hiring one person for a managerial position at her company. She had interviewed close to 20 people for this position and had narrowed it down to two candidates. One being a younger Caucasian male who had recently earned his degree in this specialization and the other being an older African-American male who had 10 years of proven job history and success with this same company. She emphasized that this was the hardest decision she had made in her profession and felt that she chose fairly regarding whom to hire. She reported that the older African-American male had been a very hard working employee since he was hired and had demonstrated a wonderful leadership ability and work ethic. Her hesitancy was that he did not fully complete his college education and did not have a formal diploma to produce, only transcripts. He had been about six credits short of his degree.

After much deliberation, she felt that she was acting in an ethically competent way by hiring the younger, Caucasian male with a recent college degree. She explained that the job typically "suggested" (not required) a college degree and that she felt that she would be inadvertently showing too much multicultural sensitivity or favoritism by choosing the African-American candidate. This would clearly be a tough decision for many people to have to make. She was genuine and heart-felt in her desire to make a well-informed, competent, and fair decision.

As she told her story in this class, I was struck instantly by the realization that she had actually denied granting this job to the overtly right choice. There are societal normative practices that promote fairness in hiring. Though she fully intended to make a fair decision, paradoxically, these were clearly not followed in this scenario. I would like to mention that this younger Caucasian male with the college degree was also a very strong candidate, yet he did not have the work experience or leadership experience that would be required of him on a day to day basis by her own admission and opinion.

While she was proud of the decision she made, she acknowledged that this candidate's lack of experience created some concerns and anxiety for her and others. Sadly, I think that there was an energy short-circuit within her that prevented her from making a decision that felt right and one that would have been better received by others. It boiled down to the formality of having a formal degree though it was not technically required. Sadly, the fact that the African-American candidate with 10 years of experience had all but 6 credits to complete his degree, prevented the positive energy to flow naturally in this scenario.

To me, this was an example of trying so hard to make the best decision, trying to be mindful of all of the data and information available, yet not being sure what to pay attention to and what to give more weight and consideration. Sometimes our attempts to operate in fair and balanced ways can actually create end results that are not fair or balanced at all. Following energy theory requires so much more than just a basic understanding and belief system. It is certainly a complex concept that is hard to explain, let alone follow with active mindfulness. It requires a blend of all senses and an almost artistic/creative interpretation of the data we receive from our intellect, our emotions, and our intuition.

What makes this even more difficult is that we cannot always trust our interpretations because we can have false logic; our emotions can skew or magnify our perception, and intuition can often be confused for anxiety, worry, panic, or desire. It is certainly an unsettling feeling to hear that we cannot always trust the way that we think or feel. However, I am proposing that this new method of focus and guidance can be a learned skill, no different that preparing to break a board with your hand in a martial arts class. It can be intimidating at first, but with proper technique and confidence, it can be mastered fairly easily with little effort.

*Chapter 5*

# Unexpected Results

In this section, I will discuss a short circuit that occurred within me that tapped into my fear that I was an inadequate father and provider for my children. I did not realize this at the time, but I followed energy theory in a way that unexpectedly freed me from that invisible prison.

Being a father of three wonderful children, I have watched how their existence have given my life more purpose and meaning, and how I have transformed during their growth. At the time that my oldest daughter was in preschool preparing for kindergarten, I began to notice a strong building urge inside of me to provide opportunities for her to excel in her future. I even noticed internal reactions each time I drove by a local private school specializing in education from kindergarten to eighth grade.

During several trips to that area while looking for a home for our growing family, I was continually struck by the positive energy that seemed to radiate in the sky above that school. It seemed to draw me into a deep gaze and fantasy about what must be happening in "that" building. In fact, my wife and I would joke about the traffic hazard this school caused because I could not stop looking at it as we drove by. It was like some of the houses that we were shopping for at the time, the kind that you could picture your children growing up in and watching a movie clip of your grandchildren coming for a visit for holidays and special occasions.

Yet, there was something weighing very heavy in my heart simultaneously during that experience. I thought of it as an impasse between having tasted from a cup of divinity, wanting to provide my children with the most enriching opportunities, versus the harsh realization of our financial limitations. Despite my wife's realistic protest, I felt that it was important to go on a tour of the school to find out more information. After our initial visit with the admissions director, I quickly realized how much this school was really outside of our reach. This realization was saddening and embarrassing to me as I looked into my daughter's eyes, knowing how special she is and what she is capable of, yet also knowing our financial limitations. This realization almost led me to decide not to submit the application. However, I did not believe in self-defeating thoughts and actions. Being a person who listens to intuition, it was important for me to be able to create a forum to share with the dean of the school and the admissions director how I felt about the school and the impact that it already had on us; regardless of whether or not our daughter was enrolled.

I believed that I was following a positive energy momentum that could allow something special to occur, namely, that they would see our daughter and decide that she was just the type of student they wished to have at the school and offer us enough of a scholarship or tuition waiver to make this work. It turns out that the energy signals I followed were meaningful to me but in a completely different way than I would have expected. The outcome was completely unpredictable and surprising.

During this process, my wife took a realistic approach that this school would not be willing to waive their $28,000 kindergarten tuition and that we were essentially wasting everyone's time in the process. She was of the belief that there was no point in investing time and energy in attending meetings and writing letters to the school administrators. The interesting thing about our relationship is that we both tend to be right and wrong at the same time but for very different reasons. However, in a very, very, rare moment, she relinquished to me and went along with the process. During our second and last visit to the school, we were able to meet with the dean himself and to review our application, our daughter's academic assessment, but more importantly, to share our hope and vision for our daughter's academic pursuits.

What happened next was nothing short of what I considered to be divine intervention. I quickly felt a strong sense of peace and a releasing of the feelings of inadequacy within me only three and a half minutes into meeting with the dean. I was struck instantly with a new perspective; my belief that the dean had an agenda and vision for the school, and for the children of our future, that posed some very alarming concerns for me. In the spirit of being respectful of other people's views and trying to avoid negativity, I will keep this brief and general. Overall, the dean's message was that he believed that academic pursuits need more world competitive focus and that business and sciences should trump the arts and creative forms of academia. In addition, he believed that part of the decline in society and in our nation's economic progress was related to an over focus of parent's listening to the needs of their children. He believed that "children do not know what they need and that it is our job to tell them"- his exact words. While I have some unconventional and radical views myself regarding the decline in society, economics, politics, and government, I feel uncomfortable about the idea of stifling the individual expression of a child's self-identity and future path. I can see some validity in the perspective that parenting has shifted perhaps a bit too far at times; I sometimes wonder if we have burdened our children by providing too many choices and too many opportunities for activities, etc. Maybe this has partially contributed to why people feel over-scheduled?

I was enamored for the duration of the meeting, not so much by what he was saying, but more so by the value of attending this meeting. As I mentioned earlier, it was quite a dichotomous experience for me to drive by the school up until this point. I coveted this school, what I thought was the energy within the building, and then felt a sense of failure as I could not afford to send my children there. My wife was correct that the school would not be willing to help us financially, but I was also correct that there was an intuitive value of going through the motions of this process. I did not know it at the time but the experience was important from a releasing standpoint for me. I came to understand that the beautiful nature of the building and the campus was, for me, merely just that. It was not illustrative of the work that I thought was being done within that building regarding nurturing our children and changing our future in a different direction. It is not my intention to sound judging or critical of this school, it is merely my attempt to showcase the importance of collecting more information and allowing yourself to go through the motion of something with a belief system that is not necessarily logical/reality based.

However, I want to also clarify that I am not suggesting to throw caution to the wind. It is important to keep a sense of openness and preparation for things that can unfold in ways that we do not expect, or that are even unpleasant at first glance. Perhaps this school remains helpful to many, perhaps that particular dean is no longer affiliated with that school, or perhaps the philosophy has changed there? In either scenario, I can drive by that school with a neutrality instead of a longing to have my children attend there, and a lesson learned about not coveting things upon a shortsighted exposure to it. It has now become a beautiful architectural building that I simply admire while driving by.

# Chapter 6

# The "Why" versus the "What"

In the previous scenario, one of the areas of focus was that it can be important to follow energy flow without a primarily logic centered approach. I knew that the experience would be important to me, but I did not know why it would be important. In fact, it became important to me in a way that I could not predict. In the next scenario, I will discuss the importance of considering "why" we do things. Why do we choose to do what we do? I believe that the "why" can often be even more important than the "what."

I have come to learn that there is not always one clear "right" answer to handling any given situation. In the hundred or so people that I have asked about the following situation, I made sure to remind people to answer genuinely based on what they would do, not what they think is the "right" answer. And, more importantly, I asked them to explain "why" they would choose one action over the other. I have consistently found that it is within this dialogue about the "why," that people come to learn and understand more about themselves. This knowledge has shown to be helpful and applicable in a variety of ways and situations to people. It has become almost invaluable in terms of what is learned in self-awareness. Please bear with me, this section gets a little complicated. I would recommend that you take your time to slowly think this out a bit.

Imagine that you are shopping in a large warehouse bulk goods-type of business that sells everything from groceries to tires to televisions. You are there to purchase a full size mattress and support box spring for a bedroom in your home. Given that this is a large warehouse bulk discounter, you have a large platform push cart to lay down the mattress and box spring. When you get up to the front cash register, the employee scans in your items, tells you a total of $250 plus tax. Something seems amiss, the price of the mattress was $250 and the box spring was $100; that should total $350 plus tax. In that very moment, the crux of the dilemma is presented. It appears that the cashier scanned the stacked box spring and mattress as one complete set. Essentially forgetting to move the mattress aside and scan in the box spring separately. The $250 figure was for the mattress while the $100 box spring was left off of the bill.

In this brief millisecond you have to decide how you want to handle this situation. For some, this is not a dilemma or a hard decision at all, the choice is clear based on their internal philosophies and external world experiences. What is your initial inclination? Please remember, try not to answer based on what you think is "right," try to answer based on what you would do. Furthermore, the "why" and rationale for this answer is most important to your self-understanding. Some would choose to simply pay what the cashier quoted, thinking that perhaps there was a discount they were not aware of, or that even being aware of this error, they would accept it as a "gift" believing it was their lucky day. The people I have asked these questions to and who answered in this way did not believe that their decision was "wrong" or unlawful. They did not feel they were being dishonest or were stealing the items. In this belief system, the simplicity of the decision was as follows:

> *I brought my items to the cashier with full intention of paying for everything that I wished to walk out with. The cashier scanned the items and told me what to pay, and that's what I intend on doing. I don't know if he/she made a mistake, it's not my fault if he/she did, and it kind of doesn't bother me because I just want to buy what I need to and leave.*

Upon further examining of this type of rationale, the people who often chose this route tended to explain that the larger bulk discount retailers are likely making large profits, would not likely notice or miss this income loss, and it was believed that they do not likely pay their employees enough anyway or should not charge a membership fee to shop at their store. This type of thought process led many people to feel justified in capitalizing on an opportunity to save money.

Conversely, there tended to be another belief system in which the decision was clear to some people that they would quickly notify the cashier of the error/discrepancy. In this belief system, the rationale was multifaceted as well. Initially, there was a belief that it was dishonest and wrong to knowingly allow oneself to walk out of a store not paying for an item. Regardless of the innocence of the buyer, once he/she became aware of the $100 omission, some did not feel right inside accepting what had unfolded. Quite simply, this decision was hinged upon an internal dialogue of:

> *I came here to buy this mattress and box spring set, prepared to spend this money, and if I walk out of here not paying for the box spring, then I am stealing it. I may even get caught at the front door when they check receipts on the way out. And, I do not wish to contribute to a decline in humanity in our society or economic collapse due to larger corporations trying to offset their losses by increasing prices or not paying higher wages to the employees. I want to do my part and be as honest as I can.*

So far we have mapped out a split between two options for how to handle this dilemma based on a specific internal belief system. Now let us take a look at an issue of <u>consistency</u> versus <u>flexibility</u> based on new information. Regardless of how and why you would handle the above scenario, let us imagine that one year later you find yourself in need of an additional mattress and box spring purchase for another room. You have enjoyed the quality and the price of the previous product thus far and return to the same store for a repeat purchase. You are pleased to find this same mattress and box spring for sale at the same price. Ironically, you are presented with the exact same decision again at the front register. The cashier rings up your items and you notice the mathematical discrepancy. It takes you a moment, but in a flash you remember that this happened to you one year ago at the exact same store, buying the exact same thing. It certainly feels like déjà-vu, or a "glitch in the matrix," or some type of cosmic test. How do you respond this time? Is your decision the same or different? What is your rationale and justification this time?

Here we have an example of the scenario kicking it up a notch and creating a tad more of a dilemma for you. If you chose to pay the amount the cashier mentioned the first time a year ago, do you view this as a chance to do the opposite and pay this second time to balance things out? Or do you believe that this is a "gift" or opportunity to prosper because you are a good person, you work hard, and you could also use a break with the outgoing money for bills and daily living expenses. Another belief would be to pay the "correct" amount again, if you did the first time, based on the notion of consistency and the same rationale used before; namely, that it does not "feel" right.

Conversely, what if you did not pay the "correct" amount the first time and considered the unknowing discount as a gift or opportunity? In that case, do you bring the discrepancy to the attention of the cashier based on a belief that you "got away with it" once and would not want to tip the scales of karma? Or, do you decide to pay what the cashier quoted based on a belief that they continue to make mistakes that you are not responsible for? Namely, that you are being an honest customer by bringing your items up to the front and paying what you are being asked to pay.

The justification for this decision adds another layer to this simple hypothetical ethical dilemma. What do your answers depend upon? Your mood that day, the friendliness of the cashier or lack thereof? If someone cut you off on the road on the way home from work? This is why I believe that it is vital to have a self-understanding/mindfulness of how you operate, why, and what information you use and pay attention to in order to make decisions that you can live with.

I want to thank you for hanging in there to consider the multifaceted steps to this complex scenario. The thing that stands out to me about being in this situation is how the temptations can be dangled in front of us, creating challenges for us to operate consistently regardless of outside influence. Or, how the temptations can be dangled in front of us to create opportunities to adapt and to be flexible. In either case, if one does not have an acute awareness of how he/she operates and why (self-understanding), then there is an extremely high likelihood of making a decision that will lead to some type of negative consequence. Most likely, an internal consequence of feeling like you made an incorrect decision, a scenario which will most definitely lead to anxiety, concern, and self-doubt.

I have heard many rationales and justifications from people regarding this scenario. There were a significant amount of people that would never bring these errors to the attention of the store, feeling justified that they rarely profit from their own kindness and law abiding actions. But what is missed in this justification? There are other things to consider than just the self, what about the employees, the business investors and their families, or even the other customers who will eventually have to pay more for their products to offset the financial losses of the store? On the other hand, there were a portion of people that would bring these errors to the attention of the stores. They quickly felt that it was the correct and humane thing to do. But what is missed in this justification? What about the fact that sometimes good things can happen to good people, that perhaps this was presented to them three times for a reason, what about the "gift" mentality that there are cosmic and karmic earnings that can be cashed in upon?

The scenario described above was absolutely a true story and happened to me several years ago. It was so odd that it stayed with me and I felt compelled to find out how other people would approach the situation. I will share with you my decisions in the moment and more importantly, my rationale. On a side note, I am not entirely sure what this means but I have not run into another person who answered similar to myself. I would not profess to have handled this in the best way possible, but I do strive to operate in creative and counter-intuitive ways.

When this occurred the first time, I was purchasing my oldest daughter's first "big girl bed." It was a symbolically significant purchase, marking the milestone of graduating from a small toddler bed to a larger and higher single bed. When I was told the lesser amount to pay than expected, I needed a moment to process what was occurring. My wife then looked at me and whispered "what should we do?" I was of the mindset that it would be great to save $100 because I was struggling to turn my business into a financially stable practice that could support my family. My wife and I have historically disagreed about the expenses of raising children. Namely, the difficult nature of her position as a stay-at-home mother and my position as a sole income provider struggling to start a practice. Those were some very tough days; but I digress. Despite my strong urge to pay what I was asked to pay and leave, I decided to bring this to the attention of the cashier. While that was not clearly a unique decision, I believe that the rationale was in fact such. I did not consider whether it was right or wrong, whether I would get caught, or whether I could use this money in other ways. What most occurred to me is that I did not "earn" that money/$100 discount. I have a strong sense of pride in giving 100% and pride in an honest hard day's work.

I have been known to help strangers on the side of the road change a tire, hold doors open for people, or help elderly people lift heavy things into their cars. I do this, not for money or accolades, but because I believe in the spiritual nature of doing such things. If I had done that earlier in that same day, I believe that I would have likely accepted that error at the cash register as a cosmic gift. I do not wish to profit from random acts of kindness, but I may have considered this opportunity as part of a way to bring positive energy back to me if I had just put out positive energy.

In the second stage of this scenario when I was faced with the same initial dilemma again, this became even more enticing to me. It occurred to me that this just does not normally happen and I could not ignore the irony or symbolism in buying this same item from the same store and being offered this same opportunity. I was convinced that this was clearly a message for me to be granted the chance to save $100. What other explanation could it be? My wife looked at me again with the same question, "what should we do?" Was this further justification to pay what they ask and to walk away, because I did not do that the first time, or was this temptation kicking it up a notch to test me? I was not sure so I took a brief moment while I held up the line to think. The cashier asked me if there was anything wrong and I said "yes, if I am not mistaken, the box spring did not get rung up." I found it very difficult to allow those words to escape my lips. Again, I did not consider the typical things that led many people to the same choice. Instead, I thought to myself, "what if this was a test and I need to be cautious as to how to proceed?" I decided that the universe has a tendency of balancing things out; I did not want to cosmically risk what may occur if I left the store with a belief that I had a $100 worth of "extra" money. The elation I would feel inside concerned me because I would have some superstitious thoughts like getting a flat tire on the way home or worse. Perhaps this was a test for me to either pass or fail? I was not willing to take that risk, so I told the cashier about the discrepancy for the second time.

To take this even further, when I got home I realized that I did not actually need this second box spring. The bed that we were buying this for was constructed differently than the first bed. It turned out that I could return it, thus saving $100. I was very pleased with my decision to tell the cashier about the mistake because I now had a receipt to return the unneeded box spring. I was convinced that this was the "prize" for operating consistently and resisting the temptation, though I would not judge someone for choosing differently.

On my way back to return the unneeded item, I was thinking about how rare this experience was and I pondered the meaning behind such uncanny events. I was also grateful that I chose to pay for the item because I would have been stuck and not able to return the box spring otherwise. However, I did decide that I would not want to have the extra box spring laying around and would not want to profit from it. If it turned out that I did not pay for it and was faced with a decision as to what to do, given that I did not have a receipt to return it, I decided that I would have brought it back to the store, propped it up against the customer service desk, and then would have left the store without a word.

When I arrived back to the store, I walked up to the customer service desk with the large box spring in hand to start the return process. I handed over the receipt and explained that it was unused and nothing was wrong with the box spring. Since I paid in cash, they began the process and started to count out my refund. At that time, I was still pleased with my decisions and rationale, while marveling in the uncanny dilemma of this entire ordeal. I wondered about the energetic and cosmic implications and felt very relieved that it was all over. This, of course, was until a new third layer to this story unfolded. The customer service cashier handed me $250 for my refund, not the $100 that I was expecting from the box spring.

I stood there again, paralyzed for what felt like minutes, pondering what to do. I realized that the cashier did not notice that it was the box spring being returned and assumed it was the $250 mattress to be returned. In general, I take pride in my consistency and allowing very little external triggers to change my course (but not in a rigid way). So, I paused for another moment. I was extremely tempted to accept this extra money and walk away with the mentality that this could not be an accident that this store tried to give me hundreds of dollars combined on three separate occasions. However, I decided to bring this error to the attention of the cashier again. I felt a strong urge to not allow this temptation to make my decision and felt that for just the consistency satisfaction alone, it would be worth the decision to correct their error.

In the mattress scenario above, there were three levels of opportunities presented to me during those trips to the store. The first one was whether or not to profit by receiving a free box spring. In this scenario, I operated based on the fact that I did not feel that I deserved a credit in this way. The second one was the same opportunity to accept a free box spring. In this scenario, I operated based on the fact that I did not want to evoke a negative energy circuit if this was a test and if I failed. And, the third was whether or not to accept extra money from an refund for an incorrect item.

In this scenario, I operated under the guiding principles previously described that kept me on focus and that prevented me from taking advantage of the situation.

I left the store and began asking people how they would have handled the situation. I continue to believe that there is not a clear right or wrong answer or approach in this scenario. There are approaches that offer more risks than others; there are approaches that that may lend themselves to feeling guilt/remorse; and there are approaches that may push the limits of what is socially acceptable or common. Overall, I believe that this scenario serves as a good example of the complexity within the subtle nuances of every decision made, every action or reaction, and in the ripple effect that occurs in the aftermath.

The difficult task when making decisions within the context of energy theory is deciding how to read the energy of the circumstances. We can make decisions based on the belief that there are energy signals around us that are designed to help and guide us. In this philosophy, we have a responsibility to determine if these signals are present to help us either achieve something, gain something, or perhaps to help us avoid something. Another layer to consider regarding decision making is a concept of creating an energy ripple effect. Namely, the thought and belief that operating in a proactive energy momentum can have domino effect on other things or other people. This, in turn, can even have a return effect on us, whether that be of a positive or negative nature.

Sometimes, it is important to consider the ripple effect of a decision and being mindful of protecting yourself or others; having a mindset that you can proactively build some form of an energy "credit." A credit or investment of energy that can be used at a future time. It can be unclear in the moment what all of this means and how to follow these signs and signals. The main goal at first would be to bring these concepts into your conscious awareness. By being mindful of such things, we allow ourselves much more control and protection, as well as, much more comfort in the decisions we make and why we make them.

## Chapter 7

# The Responsibility of Meta-Messages

In this next section, I would like to continue the discussion about meta-messages and the themes that are actually being communicated on an emotional level. I have mentioned briefly that a meta-message can be defined as what is actually being communicated at a higher level beyond the content of what is actually being said. Or to phrase another way: the message within the message. This concept can be difficult for people to accept because people are often unaware of the meta-messages they send, especially the negative ones. A meta-message can often be too difficult to "own" if it sounds harsh or abrasive. Namely, if that was not their intention or not what they were consciously thinking inside. In that case, the negative meta-message is viewed as clearly wrong or wrongfully interpreted. However, after years of working with couples doing relationship counseling, and after 19 years of a relationship with my wife, I have learned that small components of our communication can quickly and sharply take on a life of its own. We have a level of responsibility in what gets communicated, how it gets delivered, how accurate our messages are, and even in how messages are received. Regardless of what we mean to say, we need to exercise mindfulness in what actually happens once we say something out loud. In addition, it is important to be mindful about our own internal emotion and intention before something is said.

Consider very briefly a scenario in which an energetic 5 year old comes downstairs to greet his parents with a pride the he picked out an outfit to wear all by himself. The outfit does not match and the parents inevitably mention something like "that shirt doesn't match your pants; go back upstairs and change because you can't leave the house like that." While it may be a true statement by the parent(s), and while I am not professing that a 5 year old is always capable of making the best decisions on his own, there is an important missing component here. The meta-message became, "you don't know how to dress, I will not allow you to make this mistake and have people see you like this, go fix it now!" Perhaps another approach could be, "Wow, I see that you are excited about getting yourself dressed. How do you think you look? Some people may think this outfit does not match but you can decide how important that is to you. I would be happy to help you if you would like me to."

Even though I consider myself to be a mindful individual, I will outline a brief interaction between my wife and I in which I accidentally destroyed her excitement and positive energy of a successful weekend neighborhood yard sale. I consider this to be a catastrophic failure on my part. This represents the short circuit that can occur when a person (typically a male) believes that it would be good to try to discuss the logic of a series of events. And, the subsequent ripple effect on the other person (typically a female) being left to feel misunderstood and that her intentions, both noble and pure, were "not good enough" for her beloved partner.

My wife prides herself on her ability to sell items from our children that are no longer needed in order to re-invest in new things such as clothing, toys, etc. I see it as the ultimate form of recycling. In her preparation for a local yard sale, she had spent a lot of time in the days before collecting items, organizing, pricing and tagging, and coordinating deals with our children about how any profits will be allocated. In this pursuit, she asked me if I had anything that I wished to sell. I did in fact have two boxes of old music CDs that I have converted to electronic form. There were about 200 in total and I was preparing to make a donation to the local Goodwill store. We decided that it would be worth trying to sell them at the yard sale. We went over a fun game plan for pricing and negotiating based on recent experiences of watching TV programs that show pawn shop negotiations and people who buy and sell antiques, etc.

It was fun and we both looked forward to how her day would unfold. It was my position to sell the CDs at just about any cost and to unload whatever we could. I stopped by towards the end of her day to help put things away and she was very excited to tell me that she sold all of the CDs to one buyer; the entire set, both boxes. She proceeded to tell me the story of how the person approached her, stating that he was a buyer and seller of CDs and would be willing to take them off her hands for $40. I paused for a moment when she told me this to think through what my response would have been if it were me (I do that a lot apparently), and in that moment of silence, took the wind out of her sail. She asked what was wrong and I replied "nothing, I just thought you were going to practice your negotiating skills and try to sell the CDs for around .50c/piece" (a $100 target goal). She had initially wanted to try to sell them for $2/piece but I suggested that it was important to unload them and that I didn't think they were worth more than the .50c/piece price. She said that she was sorry if I was upset or wasn't happy with her decision and, in that very moment, I knew that I had inadvertently shifted her very excited and happy energy to a deflated energy and her feeling inadequate. Sadly, this is a very good example of how the intention to discuss logic, can accidentally destroy or hurt another.

She explained that she was excited because she was able to sell all of the CDs and thus accomplished the goal of unloading all of them at once, since they were going to be donated anyway. She was absolutely right about that success, and while I was not upset, I was a little confused by my perception that she did not follow through with <u>her</u> original plan. We both had valid points, and I tried very hard to present my thoughts neutrally, but alas, I got short circuited in a millisecond and ignored her excited emotion due to my initial logical thought and confusion about the change in her strategy. This must have upset her on quite a deep level because she awoke early the next morning, not typical for her Sunday morning routine, and was thinking about what she perceived to be my disappointment. She apologized again for not selling the CDs for more money and I felt a profound sense of guilt and failure that I really miscommunicated and took away all of her fun from that day. For me, this was certainly not about money, as I was originally prepared to donate them. It was more so about what a fun plan we came up with and her being able to practice what we watch on TV.

Some may say that she was too sensitive in this example and did not really listen to the fact that I said I was not upset and was just curious as to what unfolded. It was clearly me who has missed the cue initially in what to pay attention to and how to match her excitement and hear more details about her day. It got derailed quickly with my simple pause and I could not stop the trajectory. That is how critical the subtle nuances of communication can be. If I followed the energy better, I would have been able to balance nurturing her excitement while still having a dialogue about my attempt to understand things. There would have been adequate time for me to ask my questions and to understand more about what unfolded after I first shared in her excitement and success.

# Chapter 8

## Truth and Meta-Messages

The following is another important example regarding the delicate nature of being attentive to the needs of others, while also being truthful, genuine, and not compromising yourself in the process. There are many opportunities that we are constantly faced with that illustrate such dichotomies. Let us consider the following example in more depth; how to handle answering this question from a child "Is Santa real?" In an effort to operate in extreme mindfulness (a tiring task for many parents), I have some suggestions about addressing such provocative questions from such special and intuitive little beings.

If you are reading this you are certainly conscious of the importance of nurturing and supporting the intuition and spirituality of others, especially with the little ones. If you cringe hearing the statement; "our dog didn't die, he went to live at the farm," or "he just went to sleep for a very long time," then it is my hope that the following example will resonate with you and will help with how to address the dilemma of handling sensitive philosophical questions. These questions require answers that hold a delicate balance between allowing a child's innocence and imagination to linger in the realm of fantasy and age appropriate dose of genuine truth.

As each Christmas holiday approaches, we start to notice the television commercials depicting competition between professional shopper moms and Santa. These commercials showcase a subtle internal struggle within parents and the holiday season. Certainly, it is a widely held belief system that holidays have become more commercialized over the years, drifting vastly from the religious, spiritual, and traditional intended origins. With that said, another problematic dynamic that occurs for parents is the notion that they work very hard throughout the entire year, waiting to be the hero in their children's eyes to provide their little ones with the current coveted "thing." Parents often save their hard earned money, sacrificing other purchases, and even going into debt to make sure that their children have a great holiday season; namely as depicted by the quality and quantity of presents. For many, there is an existential resentment that their hard work, sacrifices, and efforts to be the hero often get sidelined because a child may believe in Santa and assign credit to the white bearded stranger.

Parents often enjoy this time of year and the innocence in their children's beliefs. However, there is also often an inner frustration that Santa gets to be the hero and they cannot allow themselves to destroy the holidays due to their own ego of wanting to feel important and appreciated by their children. A child's belief in Santa, or the Tooth Fairy, or the Easter

Bunny is sacred in some ways; but it also seems to overshadow the gratitude he/she may have toward their loved ones who care for them so much and who provide for them throughout the year. It is hurtful to many parents who want to provide for their children but also do not want to over provide (spoil) and contribute to a child's unawareness of the value of the dollar. The age old saying "money doesn't grow on trees" seems to be a fitting statement that comes to mind.

Moving forward, I have a suggestion that offers a solution to the dichotomy between not wanting to deceive our children and not wanting to bring them into an adult reality before they are ready. I am essentially referring to the unintentional meta-messages that can create internal conflict and confusion. As previously mentioned, a meta-message can be defined as the underlying message of what is really being communicated. Consider this example "You need to take your shoes off, go upstairs, brush your teeth, and get into bed." The unintended meta-message is "I will tell you what you need because you are not capable of knowing this and deciding it for yourself." If you read this and disagree with the meta-message, consider the subtle difference in restating "you need to…." vs. "I need you to…." or "can you please take your shoes off, etc."

But, I digress, let us not forget Santa. I propose an alternative to the all or nothing style belief systems regarding the idea of Santa. I believe that there is something in between the two very polarizing positions that either Santa is a real person who circles the globe faster than the speed of light or that Santa and the spirit of Christmas is fake and not meaningful. I propose that there is an approach that can be blend being "real" and honest with an approach that would not destroy the innocence of childhood by admitting Santa is fabricated.

I suggest true honesty about the symbolism of what Santa represents in terms of Christmas and gift giving. The concept that we use our imagination and fantasy to describe the idea of spreading joy to others and the value of giving from the heart. In addition, the notion of receiving the gift of humanity and inner peace through the act of giving, regardless of religious beliefs and participation in religious holidays. Sadly, as a society we have transitioned into giving out of obligation, out of guilt, out of commercialism and consumerism. Sadly, we have unintentionally betrayed the trust of our children by not answering their questions in an honest, mindful, open, and intelligent manner; just like with questions of God and death. When we make statements that Santa ate the cookies and put presents into the stockings etc, we actually run the risk of stifling philosophical imagination, spiritual growth, and exploration in children. I recognize that it may not seem like the case because it is our attempt to foster imagination and fantasy in our children by making these statements.

However, by not giving children more information to ponder, any further exploration by them tends to cease.

It is not likely that at age 15 or at age 25 people will be resentful towards their parents for the "lie" of Santa, the Tooth Fairy, and the Easter Bunny. Yet, it does represent a fracture that occurs in the subconscious belief system about what children can address with their parents about the world and their beliefs. Sadly, we fail them by denying and dismissing their intuitive doubt and thus leave them feeling a subconscious and existential void/hurt because they were led to believe that their intuition is wrong. Then, one day they realize that their intuition was right….but it is too late at that point to foster their intuitive self and it is too late to make up for the "betrayal."

At first glance, this new philosophy may sound anti-Santa, and anti-allowing children to remain in childhood innocence, yet it is actually designed to foster greater imagination and expansive thinking which can allow for a closer connection to what Santa and Christmas represent for those who participate in that holiday and tradition.

Children have a remarkable intuitive sense of the world they experience, much more than we give them credit for. So, here is a sample of what I think offers children a blend of honest and informative information from their parents mixed with a continued belief in magical and unexplained things that occur in the world/universe. It is my belief that it nurtures children, encourages exploration and questioning, and validates their intuitive sense. A sense that tells them something does not seem right about one person being physically able to circle the globe in one evening, entering homes of children throughout the world, knowing their names, and if they have been naughty or nice, all in one evening. The following is a sample dialogue.

Child: Is Santa real?

Parent: That is a great and complicated question. I'm glad that you are thinking about Santa and trying to figure out what you believe, I'm sure that you have heard a lot of different things about Santa. Let's see if we can help you to decide what is "real" to you. Some people believe that Santa represents the "spirit" of Christmas, the idea of gift giving to show love and appreciation for those that mean so much to us, and even for those that we do not know. Kind of like showing respect and consideration for all people. Sometimes that's a very complicated thing to explain and it helps to use our imagination to come up with an image and symbol which represents those ideas. So, is Santa a real person that flies in the air in a sleigh pulled by reindeer? Well, not literally, but what Santa represents is very real. In some ways, Santa is in all of us that feel the spirit of Christmas. The great thing about being your age is that you can use your imagination and fantasy to believe in Santa to explain the importance of Christmas and what gift giving is supposed to be. So, how do we define what is real? Is it something that you can see or touch? Well then how do we know that love is real or that the Internet is real? We feel it, we believe it, we see what we think are the signs and evidence that it exists. So, you tell me, is Santa real to you?"

Perhaps this can offer a template for a new discussion that balances honoring the trust children put in us mixed with fostering creative, intuitive, and spiritual awareness in our children. Or, perhaps we can just laugh at the holiday commercials suggesting competition with Santa and just ignore this dilemma?

*Chapter 9*

# What to Pay Attention To

It is very difficult to distinguish between what is an accurate intuition or signal to follow versus what is simply an impulse or an emotional reaction, which may not be the healthiest inclination. More often than not, we are faced with dilemmas multiple times per day that challenge us and require split second decisions. This mostly occurs on a subconscious and instinctual level. When we actively pursue mindfulness, self-awareness, and the exploration of ourselves and others, we can feel a tad overwhelmed and paralyzed. This can eventually lead to an existential internal crisis. We can second guess, doubt our decisions, over analyze, and be left with feelings that rock our foundation and threaten our stability. Sadly, this can be a side effect of such pursuits. However, as with any new found skill, it takes time to acquire and master the individual components of that skill and to put it together into a cohesive and complete way of thinking, being, and behaving.

Thus, we are left with the question of "what do we pay attention to?" This is a complex question, but there is a simple answer; we pay attention to "everything." This answer in and of itself likely creates anxiety or frustration just by hearing it. It does not provide any relief or peacefulness and more so evokes further questions of, "How can I cope with everything?" "Won't that just make me feel crazy?" Or, "How is that supposed to help me when I am trying to not over think or be stressed out?" These are all very legitimate questions, but I would add to that first answer with this statement "pay attention to everything but be affected by very little." While we are paying attention to everything, we should also simultaneously acquire the skill to assess what is actually worthy of our continued efforts or thoughts. Namely, we need to build our "triage" skills and then learn to focus on prioritizing our energy/resources, filing things in appropriate categories, etc. There is a saying for those who practice active substance abuse recovery. It is called the serenity prayer, and I think that it is fitting to help illustrate this concept. "God grant me the serenity to accept the things I cannot change, the courage to change the things I can, and the wisdom to know the difference."

The wisdom to know the difference is part of the key element of paying attention to everything but allowing yourself to be affected by very little. If we train ourselves hard enough, it will be become an automatic process; to be vigilant and mindful, yet to not allow those observations and external things to derail us or "short circuit" us. It is a difficult task, but it is a simple concept. Consider this example for a moment.

You are at a restaurant with a small group of people. The server comes by the table to take everyone's drink order. You are the last one asked and you have decided that you would like an iced tea. The server asks if you would like that sweetened or unsweetened and you reply that you would like sweetened tea. The server leaves the table and you resume your conversation with your party. As the server returns in a few minutes, he/she starts to put down everyone's drink in front of them. When it is your turn you are told:

"I'm sorry but the sweet tea machine is broken. They are working on fixing it and, if they get it fixed, I'll bring out the sweet tea you ordered. In the meantime, here is an unsweetened tea."

If this is the only information you have so far, what do you pay attention to in this example? How you do you think or feel about the server bringing out an unsweetened ice tea? How do you handle the situation? We are processing these questions instantaneously as it is occurring and we will all likely have different answers. Some will feel frustrated that they were not brought what they ordered. Some would feel that it was presumptuous of the server to bring out something else and would have preferred the choice/option of another drink. Some would look at the server's intentions as a good effort in customer service; "at least she did not come back empty handed, she brought me the closest thing that was available." Some may feel the pressure of drinking the unsweetened tea as to not feel wasteful. And some, may sweeten the tea themselves at the table and move on with the conversation.

Using energy theory in this way, I would advise a holistic approach that would include this internal dialogue. Please note that it is does not have to be this lengthy, but I would like to elaborate for clarity purposes. Once proficient, this internal dialogue can occur within moments of watching this scenario unfold and one can arrive at the following conclusion rapidly:

> *I ordered an unsweetened tea and I am a little disappointed that the machine is broken, but I am grateful that the server tried to bring me the next closest thing-so as not to delay my drink as I watch others enjoy their order. I can either order something else, because I am not obligated to do anything, or I can adapt and drink this tea as is, or I can add my own sweetener. Either way, I am here to have a nice meal and to enjoy the company of the people I came with. This is not an act against me and I do not wish to allow this to occupy anymore time or energy.*

Unfortunately, I had observed this very incident in the past and had a front row seat to how this derailed and upset the person who was disappointed by not getting his drink order. The sticking point for this person became "but I didn't order this tea." Despite the server's several attempts to acknowledge the person's frustration and to offer alternatives, it seemed to deflate the person's ability to adapt and to put this incident into perspective. Interestingly, the person recovered after a five minute lapse, but it seemed to change the mood of the table and it diminished the positive sentiment of what the experience was intended to be.

As mentioned earlier, it can be very difficult to know what to pay attention to and what to respond to in scenarios. There is no clear right or wrong in this. However, it is important to look at several perspectives. I have asked many people about their reactions to the previous scenario. One person worked as a server in another establishment and she answered the question from the perspective of the server. She posited that it is considered poor customer service to come back to the table empty handed, and therefore, more proper to come back with something. Yet, she added that it would have been her decision to bring back a water as the sweetened tea replacement instead of the unsweetened tea. By choosing this route, her philosophy was that she would come back with something for the customer, but it would be a more "neutral" drink that someone at the table would likely use and the customer would not feel as badly about either "wasting" the drink or feeling obligated to drink it anyway. I noted that her choice in this scenario was very unique and likely to offer the most successful outcome for a variety of customers.

If we consider the previously suggested mantra to paying attention to everything but to be affected by very little, we can use the tea example as a template for creating anchor points in our energy. Certainly, people are free to think and feel in any way that they chose. It is also important to expand that to the thought that people cannot always control what they think and feel; sometimes thoughts and feelings can be immediate and subconscious with very little mindfulness. The caveat to this concept is that it is helpful for people to monitor and temper "how" they react to things and their behaviors associated with those initial internal reactions. It is not much different than the idea of speaking with a young child about hitting out of anger. We can say, "It is okay to be upset with that person but it is not okay to hit, please use your words to tell them that you are upset."

Regarding the tea scenario, there is no problem with the idea that a person would be frustrated or disappointed if the drink he/she ordered were not available; or, to feel stuck when another drink was brought to him/her without being given a choice. The main point here is that, when using energy theory, one can achieve some peace and sense of control by evaluating the other levels and dynamics that could be occurring simultaneously. That may offer a moment or two to regroup internally and to work on the "triage" skill of "what am I going to allow in my external world to upset me or to influence me?" Hopefully, with more and more practice, the answer to that question becomes "I am not willing to allow much to upset me or to influence me." Perhaps a difficult task at times but certainly a simplistic concept.

## Chapter 10

# What to Allow to Influence You

This section may sound contradictory to the concept of being affected by very little, but I would like to clarify that being affected by very little does not imply being cold, distant, non-caring, or inept. In fact, it is important to allow yourself the flexibility of adapting to new situations, new information, or the energy of others. We seem to have to make very calculated decisions while we are processing new data on a constant basis. We are human and we certainly have emotional reactions to things, both positive or negative. I believe that there needs to be a balance between our own internal grounding and our ability to follow the signs and signals that may serve as cues (or opportunities).

The first step in working towards this skill is to cultivate a philosophical openness to hearing and listening. This includes the belief that we can learn from others regardless of our differences in age, gender, race, ethnicity, religion, etc. In addition, it includes an openness to taking in information beyond our five basic senses. Namely, to think in energetic, intuitive, creative, spiritual and oftentimes unconventional ways. This is certainly an acquired skill that takes time and patience to cultivate. We will need constant internal reminders and redirection during this philosophical transition. There will be times of frustration in which you will not feel that this approach is "working." To be honest, that is likely when you are right in the middle of an important shift. The key to success in adopting this type of thinking is to keep an openness within yourself that you may not know the answers, that your perceptions and emotional reactions could be influenced by past experiences, and that there are greater sources of wisdom and knowledge in this universe besides your own thought process. We are evolving and adapting every day; humility in our mind and heart regarding this concept is very crucial.

There was a time in the not so distant past when I was working with a teenage young man regarding his impulse control, his anger management within his family dynamics, and being mindful about his decision making. He was a remarkable young man because he was certainly unconventional in every sense of the word. He was an enigma. On paper, he had a track record that indicated an extremely problematic behavioral pattern. School trouble, conduct issues, substance use, and some other mild law violations. Typically, people would interpret someone with this kind of track record as a very disturbed individual in need of major redirection. While that view is valid, there was another side to him, a side that few had an opportunity to see. He was extremely compassionate toward others-helping strangers and the elderly when he could and standing up for his friends. He was creative artistically and even more so mechanically. He developed mechanical skills at a young age and began to cultivate business ideas instead of the conventional idea of working at a local store to earn a minimum wage. It became evident to me very early on during my work with him that he was a very special individual, destined for something very important in this world. He required unconventional intervention, parenting, and guidance.

One of my favorite things about him was a dichotomy between two competing themes within him and effects he had on other people. The first theme was his ability to "melt" a person's brain with frustration from him pushing his/her buttons. Yet, the second theme was his ability to warm a person's heart, making that person feel very grateful to know him. In addition, he did not seem to intentionally decide how he would interact with people. He was not calculating and actively manipulative in that way. In my belief system, he could not consistently harness his energy in a productive manner. He felt so much, he thought too much, he got overloaded and overwhelmed (though he would never admit feeling that way) and he found himself mostly in a reactive state. He could not manage his "superpowers" very well. This became my primary area of focus with him. He was a very likable young man, good looking, social, popular, talented, and his family was so loving and supportive of him. They were the type of people that he needed as parents. His spirit would have been stifled and perhaps destroyed if he lived in a home in which he was constantly bombarded with enforcement of micro-house rules and power struggles. The family did their fair share of trying to hold him accountable for his behavior and not allowing him a carte blanche style living.

The concept of harnessing a "superpower" will be discussed more extensively later in this book. For now, I wish to describe how this young man influenced me in a way that perhaps saved my life. I ride a motorcycle to work throughout the entire year on most of the days of the week. My commute is short, I have winter warmth gear, and I have fallen in love with riding so much that I ride in as low as 20 degree weather. This young man had a passion for all types of vehicles and we have discussed various mechanical repairs, modification ideas, and important concepts for him to keep in mind as we guided him to the idea of starting his own repair business one day.

On a side note, I do most of the mechanical maintenance on my vehicles myself and enjoy the satisfaction of a job well done, figuring out and diagnosing mechanical problems, saving money in the process and the ease of mind in knowing my attention to detail. This young man shared my passion and had similar philosophies in those regards. I had planned to do some basic maintenance on my motorcycle but there was not a critical rush for me. One day after the end of our appointment he mentioned that my chain seemed to need some lubrication. He just happened to notice that on his walk from the parking lot past my motorcycle to the front door. It could not have taken more than a second or two to notice something like that. I was very proud of him for his attention to detail; he will no doubt be successful in virtually any of his endeavors.

I took that as a signal that I needed to attend to that issue sooner rather than later. My energetic principle was as follows:

*I know that I need to set aside the time to check my tire pressure, lubricate my chain and other moving parts, and to check my brake pads and throttle cable, etc. It's very hard to do this at 9 o'clock at night, before I get a chance to eat dinner. And, it's hard to do this on the weekends because my primary goal is family time and activities. However, I am open to being influenced by the universe or by people under certain conditions and circumstances. In this instance, this young man was right that I needed to do this and since I have now heard that from an external source-when I was already planning to do it, it now has to come as top priority. There must be a reason for hearing that message now and for hearing that message from him. I connect with him and I value his opinion.*

So after I got home that night, I ate dinner and went out to attend to the first and simple task of lubricating the chain. In the process of doing that, I noticed that the chain was very loose. It was rubbing against the chain guard and it had about 4 inches of vertical slack/play. The specifications allow for about one inch of travel. To a person like me, this is very important and I was grateful for that find. In my opinion, I need that bike to operate and perform exactly as it should, there is no room for error with something as dangerous as riding a motorcycle. I do not take that risk lightly. I am not exactly sure what could have happened at the wrong moment if that chain popped off or broke in traffic. It could have been life threatening in all honestly. If it were not for his observation about the chain needing lubrication, I would not have noticed the tension problem/slack for quite some time. I do not exaggerate when I say that he could have helped to save my life. Though he was not aware, I felt a strong urge to follow the energy of this scenario in the exact moment that he made his comment. I knew it would be vital to attend to this one matter right away.

Regarding the question of "what to allow to influence you?" Well, that depends on several things: an openness to following signs and cues presented to you, an openness to being flexible and adapting to new information and people around you, and using your creativity to blend information from your five senses, as well as, your intuition. In addition, the intent, the energy, and the method of approach from the people that communicate with you also should be considered. In the situation above, I knew that he was right in his observation, though neither of us knew the severity of it. It was simply clear to me that I needed to attend to the chain that very night because, in my opinion, energy theory dictated that this was what needed to happen. I believe that the discovery of the more dangerous issue with the chain was validation of following energy theory. To further follow energy theory principles, I also knew that it would be an open energy loop until I gave him and his family feedback on what happened.

They had just left for a family vacation and there was a small crisis that almost prevented this trip from occurring. The crisis included toxic communication between this young man and his parents, surrounding another series of behaviors that pushed boundaries and limits and that indicated an uncontrolled and risky operating system by him. He is certainly the type of young man that people care about and want him to succeed. It is frustrating to the adults around him when he escalates his risky behaviors and thus potentially threaten to change the course of his future and his wonderful potential. We spent some time in family counseling just before they left for the trip, trying to regroup and rebuild the trust and peace within each person and between them interpersonally. The family was accustomed to getting phone calls about this young man on a fairly frequent basis. These calls were not often about the positive things he did or the positive impact he has had on another.

I felt compelled to call them directly while they were on their vacation. When the mother answered, she had an understandably worried tone in her voice. She was not expecting to hear from me and was likely dreading the nature of my call since it caught her off guard. I started with "I need to talk to you about your son.................I don't want to bother you on your trip but I need to tell you about something he told me the last time he came in................." I allowed for some pause as she was listening intently. Her silence spoke loudly to me as if she was preparing to hear something bad. I then proceeded with "I need to tell you......that your son probably helped to save my life." I shared the rest of the story and emphasized that he was a very special young man, tapping into important things that he is not aware of, and that his potential for greatness was very strong. I knew that she often struggled with wondering why he had been so difficult since birth, how much they struggled to conceive him, how difficult she herself was at that age with her parents, and how much she had left in her to continue to parent him in this way. They were so much alike and she had that type of similar effect on people in a positive way.

She shared her gratitude for my call and said they were having a great time on vacation so far. She asked if I wanted to speak with him, I would not pass up that energetic opportunity, so I told him about the same sequence of events. He was modest, not taking much credit in this scenario, and made a joke about not getting into trouble yet on the trip. In this type of interaction, there were several important components to pay attention to and to allow myself to be influenced by. I have often found it to be very important to acknowledge when important things like this occur. It did not feel complete until I shared the importance of this extremely subtle but vital influence he had had and how easy it is for people to focus on the negative and get short circuited by the lesser significant things in life; like when this family used to argue about whether or not he got sent to the principal's office for being silly in class or if he got sent to there for some other reason.

## Chapter 11

# Manifesting

The term manifesting can be used to describe a basic philosophy and phenomenon known as the law of attraction; the idea that like energy attracts like energy. Within this dynamic, people have adapted this premise to the notion of one's ability to influence the type of energy that they draw in or attract to them. The thought behind manifesting is that if a person can translate thought into an emotion, that emotion gets broadcast into the universe like radio frequencies. After a period of time that broadcast will translate into drawing that energy back to the source. Some may also look at this concept as somewhat similar to karma. There is a book and movie that focuses on this very idea in more detail, it is called "The Secret" written by Rhonda Byrne. For the purposes of this section of the book, we can keep to the basic idea that I just described.

I think that it is important to reiterate that we are not fully in control of what happens to us. For example, it is not likely a valid belief system that a cancer diagnosis is brought on by someone's negative and toxic thoughts. Or that a victim of violence somehow has a responsibility in what happened, as if they elicited it somehow. There is not a clear formula or equation for how things work, or even a consensus that energy works in this way. I am a believer in manifesting energy, but I am not sure exactly how it works. In fact, I would postulate that manifesting energy works best at a subtle level, perhaps not so much as a direct desire or wish being granted so to speak, but perhaps a concept. A thought to win the lottery may translate into a feeling of prosperity and success on some other level. Or perhaps a thought to improve one's physical looks may translate into feeling loved and cared for by a partner? I have blessed to experience a tremendous success in manifesting without my direct awareness over the span of 19 years.

During my senior year of high school, I was dating my new girlfriend who had just graduated a year ahead of me. We met just after she graduated in the early summer of that year. To our surprise, we had known many of the same people but never ran into each other directly over the three years that we both attended the same school. We had concluded that perhaps there was a reason why we never met before, and that perhaps we would not have decided to date each other if we had met during those earlier opportunities. There seemed to be some type of reason why we were kept apart. During the second half of my year, I was taking an art class to finish out my some elective credits. I was asked to draw some sketches inside of a spiral note book on a weekly basis and then to write a brief description on the back.

I will fast forward for a brief moment and then pick back up with the sketch book assignment. During a recent normal family Sunday in which we play music in the house and dance around and act silly, there was something that felt familiar to me. I dismissed that feeling, convincing myself that it was simply because we usually do this on the weekends. At the time of this example, my wife was dancing in the living room with my oldest daughter, who had taken some ballerina dance lessons. They were twirling around and laughing while our oldest German Shepherd was getting in between the two of them, being a typical curious dog who wanted to join in the fun. Again, a feeling of familiarity moved over me as I watched and smiled.

About one week later, I decided to clear some things out of our basement storage area and came across my art portfolio which showcased some of my work from high school. I spent some time looking through various works of art and the memories came flooding back of what was occurring in my life and in my thoughts during each piece of artwork. I came across the sketch pad mentioned earlier and started to thumb through it while having a blankness in my memory about what I had drawn. Then, it happened in an instant. I saw an image that not only brought me to tears but it made me question my sanity for a brief moment. It was surreal. I could not believe what I was seeing, and I was not sure that the moment was real.

The sketch that had this effect on me was a drawing of a woman as she danced with her daughter in their living room. They were dancing in ballerina style near their fireplace and next to their German Shepherd. I looked at every detail in that 19 year old drawing and it all came flooding back to me. I was shocked that I had forgotten about that sketch, and more profoundly, I was shocked that I had just seen this picture play out in real life only one week before. On the back of the sketch was a description of what I wrote:

*This is a sketch of a woman as she dances with her daughter in their dream home. The woman in this picture is my girlfriend, Madeline, and she dances there in the room as she does in my mind when I think of our future together. This was just an image that I saw when I closed my eyes and thought of her.*

The similarity was uncanny. I was suddenly flooded with the emotions of when I drew this sketch. I remembered sitting in the classroom, feeling a mixture of happiness that I had such a wonderful girlfriend, and yet feeling skepticism that someone so great could really care for me. I did not have confidence in high school, suffering from extreme acne and mostly feeling like I wanted to disappear into nothingness and to not be noticed.

If I could have worn sunglasses inside the building, I would have, so as to not allow people to look into my eyes. I could not bear the thought that they could somehow read the pain I felt inside through my eyes. And, I could not bear the site of any reaction they may have had to my appearance, even if it was subtle. To me, Madeline was an angel, a beautiful girl who laughed at my jokes, made me smile, and made me feel more important than my outward appearance. When I drew that sketch 19 years ago, I was in a dark place but was being carried out of it by her. I often dreamed of our future and imagined a time in which I would feel completely happy. Even though I was only 17 years old, I knew that Madeline would change my life. I felt the power of her spirit and divinity almost instantly. She was the closest thing I had seen to God on earth at that point in my life.

I allowed myself to dream, to feel hope, and to accept the idea that my internal feeling state was not permanent and did not have to be my future reality. I drew that sketch experiencing a mixture of pain/torment with a sense of excitement and hope. I drew everything that my heart desired for my future. A beautiful wife, and gorgeous little girl, a faithful German Shepherd, a dream home with a large enough room to dance in, and a swing set peeking through the back window of that room. I drew this sketch, put it away, and completely forgot about it. Then one day, 19 years later, I felt a sensation of something that was familiar to me as I witnessed this reality unfold right in front of me. When I came across this sketch book while sorting through my old portfolio, I was paralyzed for a moment, unsure of what was happening, what I was feeling, and what to do next. I started to think about manifesting energy and the notion that perhaps this vision I kept in the back corners of my mind, and in the deep sections of my heart, somehow created a type of energy vortex that brought this into existence.

I went upstairs to show my family what I had found and they were very confused. My daughter, Abigail, asked me who drew the picture and who was in the picture. I replied that I drew it and it was of her and her mommy. Please imagine the confused look on her face as she tried to calculate and make sense out of my next response. "I drew it 19 years ago when I first met mommy." Then she replied "but, daddy, how could that be of me, I am only 10 years old?" I tried to explain this difficult concept by stating:

"I know sweetie, this is a picture of what was in my heart, something I saw in my mind when I closed my eyes. I met mommy when I was in twelfth grade and I felt so much love for her, that I could see glimpses of our future together. I could see you in your pig-tails dancing in the living room with our German Shepherds laying on the floor next to you."

She smiled but still looked as if it did not make any sense. She was certainly right about that, it did not make sense, it just does not compute when we apply any conventional thought or logic to the story. I then asked if she would be willing to dance with her mommy again in the living while I took a picture so that she could see what was so powerful about this to me. Below is a copy of the original sketch and then a copy of the picture I took right after.

To me, this illustrates the beauty and true essence of manifesting. Something that was so powerful to me at the time, something that got stored away in the memory files, yet somehow had influence to help create that very vision and bring it into reality. And yet, there is another level of profound impact and regarding this manifesting energy. The notion of the accuracy of the vision we had of our future daughter Abigail. Even that early in our relationship, we both dreamed about what our future daughter would look like and who she was going to be as person. Some may say that people can manipulate views and perception to fit various schemas and belief systems. I do believe in this psychological phenomenon. Yet, I also believe that there are things that we could not manipulate or distort in our current view of our daughter Abbie, or in a retrospective view of what we had envisioned in our past. For us, our memories remain very clear about discussions and dreams back then. We had imagined Abbie to be a bright spirit, having a profound effect on others, just like both myself and my wife. We saw her as a kind and loving person, nurturing of those around her and having a passion for life that included art and creativity, as well as a love for animals. We thought that she would be adventurous, but not reckless, and full of humor and joy.

We felt as though we were introduced to who she was, long before we decided to have children. I will never forget the internal shift inside of me one day as I changed from a position of logic/reason to that of ethereal readiness. I just started my career and was focused on trying to build my practice and gain financial stability. It was a difficult journey in that process but I was working hard to feel grounded, responsible, and ready. In my mind, there were things that I believed needed to be in place before making a decision to be a parent. Then one day, it hit me that I was waiting for something that I already had, the love and stability in my relationship with my wife, Madeline; a thing that trumped any logic of bank account numbers, vehicles to hold car seats, extra bedrooms, etc. It occurred to me that it would work out if I just kept things as simple as:

"Maddy and I love each other and we are working hard to create a life together. There is no doubt in my mind that she was destined to be a mother and that she was simply waiting on me. I do not need to let my fear get in the way of something so powerful and important to both of us. I am ready to meet our future daughter and to share our love with her."

After this realization, I experienced a deep sense of comfort and I felt as if the shift that occurred in me was guided by spirit and that Abbie was ready to be born. It did not take long for us to learn that Abbie was exactly who we had envisioned. We did not expect or predict, however, that she would have been everything we dreamed of and much, much more. Our experience of becoming Abbie's parents was indescribable for both of us. We had learned of a new level to the word, experience, and expression of "love." She gave us even more meaning and purpose in our lives and taught us so much about ourselves and each other.

We did not also expect that Abbie would have become just about the kindest older sibling any brother and sister could have had, but she did. Abbie has an almost magical effect on those around her. She guides, nurtures, teaches, attends to, and loves in a way that combines the best of both myself and her mother. Her creativity, her love of animals, and her connection to others continues to amaze us to this day. Currently, she is 11 years old, and she remains stunning in her spiritual and energetic abilities.

She inspires me and brings out the best in me, I can only hope that I never let her down, hurt her, or disappoint her.

On a side note, I never imagined myself to be one of those overprotective fathers who proclaim to not allow their daughters to date until they are 30 years old. For me, that feels dismissive of daughters' ability to make good decisions in the future, and dismissive of responsibility as a parent to guide and teach her in a way that enhances her. I remain a believer that it is my job to show her everyday how a good man acts, how he should love and respect the women in his life, and how to filter through people who are negative, hurtful, or immature. I also believe that I need to guide her but give her the autonomy to make her own decisions. I want her to feel good about the decisions she makes and to feel good about herself in the process.

Back to the notion of manifesting energy. As I look back on the few but powerful personal and professional successes in my life, it is clear to me that some form of manifesting energy has played a role in achieving these outcomes. What I am trying to suggest and illustrate here is that there is tremendous value in keeping yourself open to this type of concept. I think that it is much like what may happen when people choose to pray. Some pray with specific requests to keep family members safe, to obtain financial security, or to overcome a certain hardship. And others pray in general terms for strength, wisdom, or for divine guidance and support. In either case, people who pray do so with an internal belief that their prayers are being heard and that their prayers will be answered in some form or another, even if it is not specifically in the form of what they desire. Maybe we can approach manifesting energy with a similar belief that it is important to put it out there in the universe exactly what we are looking for, yet having an openness to the idea that things cannot always happen in the way we wish or desire. In addition, having an awareness that things are most certainly beyond our control and that we need to accept what is.

# Chapter 12

# Perception

I would like to address another interesting phenomenon about the importance that perception plays into daily activities. It is similar to the perception example described in the tea scenario in which you were asked your opinion about being brought a drink that you did not order. The more we work on expanding our perceptive skills, the more accurate we can be while navigating through things that affect us.

We often make judgments about people around us without having a lot of information about them. I believe that it happens rapidly on very subtle levels. These judgments may be accurate or inaccurate and they are based on previous experiences, our instincts, beliefs about others, prejudices, etc. Again, they may be accurate or inaccurate but they do occur fairly rapidly as we process information around us.

On a recent trip to the beach, my wife and I discovered a nice cove that had a gazebo at the end of a walkway attached to the resort where we were staying. There was a waiter setting up dinner service at a small formal table at the gazebo and we wondered about who would be dining there and why. Within a few moments we saw a woman walk up to the gazebo, she sat quietly alone at one of the chairs and gazed into the sunset while listening to the crashing waves of the ocean. We were only but 20 or 30 feet from her and our curiosity grew. In a spontaneous moment I suggested that we play a game in which we both made up a story about this person, just for fun.

My wife was hesitant to play for two reasons; the first being that it is hard for her to think of ambiguous things that are not clear, and the second being that she has grown tired of me asking tough hypothetical questions over the past 19 years. With that said, the story she made up was as follows:

"The woman sitting there is about to be proposed to. Her soon to be fiancé set up this very special dinner for the two of them and will surprise her with a ring. She is going to say 'yes' because she is in love with her partner. She will be surprised but not too much because she always knew that they would one day be married."

In my wife's imagination, this woman was waiting for her romantic partner who will assuredly make this one of the most memorable evenings of their lives. Using only the information she had at the time, my wife's feeling was of a purely romanticized fantasy, one perhaps that would have been told in a story or a movie. This was a reasonable, logical, and likely story to fill in the blanks with the information of a sunset dinner on the beach, a private gazebo dinner setting, a formal waiter at the table, and a single woman sitting at the chair.

In my imagination, I had decided that this woman was sitting at the table alone as a symbol of a relationship in turmoil (maybe I have seen too many couples in my practice as a psychotherapist?) I imagined that this woman had been the one to set up such a special and intimate dinner and that she had asked her partner to join her for dinner, as she had asked her partner to join her in life. However, the twist in my story was that she granted this invitation with the one stipulation that her partner had to straighten out some problematic and unhealthy behavior (perhaps an addiction?) I imagined that she tolerated much from this person over the years and yet still felt love and a desire to have a future together. I saw this as her last attempt to forgive and to move forward together. The partner only had to simply make the decision, a life decision, and would have to prove this commitment by showing up for this special dinner. The partner's presence would be symbolic of making that decision and choosing a life with this woman. In my mind, she sat there waiting to see what her partner would decide.

I am not exactly sure why this came to my mind, but I enjoyed filling in the blanks and using my imagination in the hypothetical. The reality of what happened next was nothing short of amazing to both us. As we continued to watch our own sunset, and while keeping an eye on our fun story time, we noticed a couple walking together in the direction of the woman seated at the table. Now this was becoming very interesting. The couple arrived at the table and we heard the seated woman say "Oh sorry, I was just sitting here and enjoying the sunset." The couple replied that it was no problem and sat down after the single woman left the area. It was clearly the couple who set up the romantic dinner and the single woman was just bold enough to take the empty chair as a spontaneous opportunity to enjoy the sunset on her own. Or, perhaps this spot triggered an amazing memory of a relationship long gone for this woman. She could have seen this empty table as a sign and the couple's arrival gave her permission to finally move on. The possibilities are endless. Either way, my wife and I had a brief laugh, and I marveled in the assumptive errors that one can make with very little information.

This example is a good illustration of the importance of collecting as much data as you can about people or a situation before making a decision. There are certainly moments in which we do not have the luxury of time to collect more information and that we may have to make quick decisions in

92

the absence of information. I believe that it is important in all situations to keep an open awareness of our limitations in our perceptions. I also believe that it is important to keep an open awareness of the things that influence our judgments and that may skew what we <u>think</u> versus the reality of what actually <u>is</u>.

# Chapter 13

## Intimacy and the Notion of Spirituality

It is well documented that there are fundamental differences between men and women in terms of how we think, feel, behave, and communicate. These differences have been the topic of religious leaders, theologians, philosophers, authors, communities, and even comedians. For the purpose of this section, I would like to focus on some of the differences between men and woman as they relate to intimacy. I believe that intimacy comes in several forms with the two main forms being emotional intimacy and physical intimacy. People often assume physical intimacy simply means sex, but that is not entirely the case. Physical intimacy can include the energy felt while in proximity to another person, as well as other forms of non-sexual touch and contact; a handshake, a touch on the arm/shoulder, a hug, or even sitting next to each other while watching TV or a movie.

In my work with couples over the years, I have found an alarming number of people who have narrowed views of what intimacy means. Many people have an extremely difficult time identifying/defining their need for intimacy, showing intimacy to their partners, and mostly, demonstrating an ability/willingness to even discuss intimacy with their partner. Sadly, it seems to be more comfortable for people to discuss intimacy with friends or even strangers rather than with the person they are most intimate with.

I would like to elaborate more on the specifics of how men and women tend to differ regarding intimacy, sexuality, and connection in communication. First, I would like to discuss a little bit of background on my spiritual and energy beliefs about women in general. In reference to the book of Genesis in the Bible, it states that "God created men and women both in his image, both male and female." Some may interpret this quite literally and some more figuratively. To me, this describes the concept that the Divine has two energy forces; one that we attribute as male/masculine and another that we attribute is female/feminine. Therefore, we could infer that there are innate qualities in both men and women that come from a single source of creation. To further this concept, let us focus briefly on the image of the Yin and Yang in Asian culture. I would not profess to be an expert on this by any means, but I offer a basic understanding beyond a common "western" view that it represents balance between good and evil or opposites. To me, it perfectly illustrates the concept of men and women being representations of complementary energy from within single source or creator.

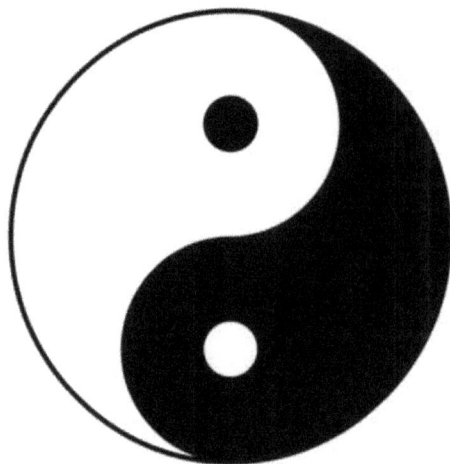

In the image of Yin and Yang, we see two beautiful shapes formed together into a circle with contrasting black and white colored sections. In each of the colored shapes, there is another smaller circle of the complementary color positioned at the core of the shape. These separate and distinct entities touch each other, forming a perfect circle (which has no beginning nor ending), and carrying deeper within its core a small component of its counterpart. Some believe the Yin and Yang to represent male and female energy and the complementary yet distinct components of each. To me, it is a very spiritual symbol that relates to the value of the opposite gender and the divinity gifted to us from a source or creator. There is an extreme importance of seeing our differences as valuable and as necessary as we try to operate in unison and harmony.

This next idea may add a tad more confusion to the mix. This may sound contradictory to the implied equality in the Yin and Yang concept and biblical references of men and women being created in God's image, but here it goes. When I think of a Creator as omnipotent- all-knowing, all-powerful, and all good, I have a conflicting thought. I believe that there is more divinity innately present in women rather than in men. This is not to say that we as men are not valuable or that we are "lesser," it is merely to illustrate the importance of women beyond what we in society typically assign to them.

I see women as examples of God on earth for a couple of reasons. The first being that women, more so than men, have a tremendous ability to create and nurture. Most notably, the female body has been designed to create, nurture, and sustain life. Regardless of whether or not a woman decides to use this ability or does not medically have this ability, she is a creator, a source of life, a nurturer, a lover, a caregiver. She is typically there for those around her, she responds to their needs, and she offers compassion and comfort. This is much like the life force energy people tap into during prayers to their God. I would like to emphasize that I used the "typically" in the previous sentence. I believe this is an inherent trait of women but I acknowledge that not all woman operate in this way. For the most part, the important people in a woman's life are cared for and attended to by her in some capacity.

Overall, I believe that these noble traits were gifted to women and were intended to give men an opportunity to appreciate God on earth and to honor the women in our lives as extremely vital to our existence, not only to our physical existence but to our emotional and spiritual existence as well. This all becomes relevant when discussing intimacy because we need to understand the different ways men and women define intimacy, show love, express themselves, and receive love. The book called "The Five Love Languages," written by Gary Chapman, is a great resource to expand on this notion. This book serves as a guide for you and your partner to discover your unique love languages and to learn practical steps towards expressing love.

How often has it been discussed that female intimacy is complicated, that men operate on a much more "simple" or primal level, and that it is hard for men to know and understand how women operate? I believe we all, women included, are susceptible to misunderstanding a woman's intentions and emotions. We will often view her actions as a result of her moodiness, her sensitivity, her "cattiness," and even her menstrual cycle or hormonal changes. I think we really do her spirit and inner self a disservice during those moments.

It is for this reason that I believe that the female energy source is like a super power. In many super hero movies, there is a person (an underdog) who acquires some form of a power. At first, they are confused by it, overwhelmed, and do not know how to control it. It often hurts the people around them and they seek solitude to "curse" this power and how they acquired it. Then, they figure out how to harness their power to help others, overcome tragedy, and even save the world. In many ways, I believe this concept is like the super power of female energy. Not every woman uses this to her fullest potential or for "good and not evil" so to speak, but for the most part, women have an innate nurturing and creative life force. Yes, she can get hurt, she can react to things in anger, and she can feel that things are worse around her than they seem to others. To use a brief example from Star Wars (I know not the most romantic of examples for women), "The Force" is comprised of the light side and the dark side. The Jedi (the good guys) work hard to control strong emotions and to be responsible with how they use the power of the Force.

But, if a woman is loved correctly, if she is attended to and cared for in a way that allows her to feel special and to feel that she is lovable despite her feelings and behavior, it unlocks "The Force" inside her; the key to her heart and her intimacy. Many men will complain about the complex nature of the women around them, the unpredictability or volatility in their emotions, and the lack of their libido or initiation of physical intimacy. However, I believe that men often look to the woman to be responsible for physical connection and intimacy. Men tend to look at sexual contact as a way to connect and as a way to relax or to operate more in unison. Often times it is the opposite for women in that when they are feeling connected, cared for, and trusting, that is when they feel comfortable being in a close, vulnerable, and giving space with their partner. This is why there can be conflicts between men and women regarding sex and intimacy. These conflicts include a woman stating that she is "too tired" or "not in the mood," and a man feeling frustrated with her lack of interest, lack of initiation on her part, or his experience of being "turned down." He will often reply with "you are never in the mood" or "then get in the mood," forgetting that he plays a role in creating the space and comfort for a woman to be in this intimate space.

Back to the concept of Yin/Yang for a moment and how this can apply to intimacy. The combination and blend of male and female energy can unlock wonderful things in how we experience ourselves, our partners, and the world around us. I believe this to be a universal concept that applies to all people regardless of their sexual orientation and identity. The concept of male and female energy should not be mistaken for literally male and female. Many of these concepts can apply to same sex relationships in that there are traits, behaviors, and perceptions that take on masculine or feminine qualities in all of us. When considering an individual, using a

Yin/Yang model, we can see that we all have a combination of these complementary energies within us.

When intimacy works well, people experience themselves as lovable, valued and valuable, desired, and as a source of joy and pleasure for their partner. That feeling generates a certain energy field each person feeds off of like a life force. It translates into their peace, communication, partnership, and many other areas of their lives outside of acts of intimacy. Furthermore, it leaves an imprint in their minds and hearts during the "in between" times of intimacy as well, aiding in the build up of the next intimate moment. When things do not work well, people are left feeling frustrated, angry, hurt, abandoned, and unimportant; which most certainly also generates another energy field. That energy field aids in further divisiveness and resentment, as well as feelings of solitude versus feelings of connection.

Let us also consider a very interesting scenario that was part of a forwarded e-mail sent to me from an unknown author. I call it the "wife's diary" and I believe that it serves as a wonderful example of the typical dynamics that unfold between a man and a woman. As you read the scenario, I want you to take note of your initial reaction to both people involved. Does one person seem to be more "right" or more "wrong?" How do you interpret the actions of each person? How does this apply to your current relationship or past relationships? And finally, what would you change, if anything, if you were in this scenario? Here it is:

-Wife's Diary:

Tonight, I thought my husband was acting weird. We had made plans to meet at a nice restaurant for dinner. I was shopping with my friends all day long and I thought he was upset at the fact that I was a bit late, but he made no comment on it. Conversation wasn't flowing, so I suggested that we go somewhere quiet so we could talk. He agreed, but he didn't say much. I asked him what was wrong; He said, 'Nothing.' I asked him if it was my fault that he was upset. He said that he wasn't upset, that it had nothing to do with me, and not to worry about it. On the way home, I told him that I loved him. He smiled slightly and kept driving. I can't explain his behavior. I don't know why he didn't say, 'I love you, too.' When we got home, I felt as if I had lost him completely, as if he wanted nothing to do with me anymore. He just sat there quietly and watched TV. He continued to seem distant and absent. Finally, with silence all around us, I decided to go to bed. About 15 minutes later, he came to bed. But I still felt that he was distracted and that his thoughts were somewhere else. He fell asleep; I cried. I don't know what to do. I'm almost sure that his thoughts are with someone else. My life is a disaster.

-Husband's Diary:

A two-foot putt.......who the hell misses a two-foot putt?

The intended humor in this scenario was a contrasting position of the wife's versus the husband's perspective. The wife's perspective was that there was a problem in the marriage while the husband's emotional distance was due to his own internal disappointment. I have noticed that people's reactions to this joke mostly gravitate in the direction that men are simple minded and that women are complicated. Namely, in this scenario, that the only things the man was focused on was his disappointment and frustration with his golf performance earlier that day. People tended to side with the husband's perspective because he told her that he was not upset and it had nothing to do with her. They felt that it was her choice to continue to believe that something was wrong and <u>her</u> responsibility that she ultimately felt an "injury." People believed that it was her perception that led her to think that he was unhappy in his relationship with her and that she has lost his heart. In addition, people have mentioned that the woman went "too far" by taking his behavior personally and went to bed crying for "no reason." You may or may not be shocked to know that this response even came from a large number of women who were asked about this scenario.

Sadly, a major point was missed in this perception, the contradiction between the statement that the man was not upset and that it had nothing to do with her. He was upset.....she was right......he just did nothing to help her see that it was over something minor that had nothing to do with her. He shows an inability to identify his own feelings in this situation. She was highly in tune with his mood and affect being the nurturer that she was. She may have misinterpreted the reasons for his mood, but she certainly sensed it. He, on the other hand, was completely unaware of his wife's growing discomfort, choosing instead to solely focus on his own thoughts.

If we take a moment to break this down, this scenario serves as a wonderful example of what plagues many relationships, the fractures in communication and misunderstandings and hurts that occur in just a few simple moments. There is a shared responsibility in how things unfolded between the two people in this scenario. To me, much of the responsibility falls onto the husband because, using energy theory, there was something that he was broadcasting about his disappointment/frustration that his wife was sensitive enough to pick up on. She intuitively knew something was amiss and made several attempts to engage him in conversation. I do believe that he has a right to not want to discuss such things and to simply be tired and distracted. However, the entire scenario would have unfolded much differently if he simply mentioned that he was frustrated about his day and that he was simply distracted and fatigued by that.

Some may say that he tried to communicate that by telling her that he was not upset and that it had nothing to do with her. However, that is not the same thing as:

"Honey, I'm sorry that I'm not talkative tonight, I'm frustrated about my day but I don't really want to talk about it. Thank you for taking the time to go out to dinner with me and to ask me how I am doing, I'm sorry that I'm just not present right now."

It is extremely likely that his wife would have appreciated his acknowledgment of her desire to connect with him. She may have felt some greater sense of comfort in that his distance was not reflective of his feelings for her or their marriage. I admit that it is not clear how much comfort she would have felt, or even if she would have accepted what he said and not made further assumptions. However, I believe that she would have felt better than how the evening did end for her. In addition, I believe that her role in this was not that she "jumped to conclusions" or took things "personally," it was that she did not voice her concern and disappointment before she went to bed that evening. I do not believe that voicing those concerns before bed is *always* the way to go, but in her case, she went to bed crying and he had no clue that she was upset, hurt, and scared. She missed giving him an opportunity to know this extremely valuable information. I also admit that it is unclear how he would have handled that or if he would have been able to be attentive to her.

The main point is that there are several layers of breakdowns in communication, there are messages sent directly and indirectly via the spoken and unspoken word, as well as through nonverbal behavior. This example serves as a reminder that each person in a communication dialogue has a responsibility in how the conversation progresses. I also believe that there are many things that can influence the outcome of a conversation before it even begins. One major factor could be the self-awareness of each individual, namely, whether the person communicating is tired, hungry, stressed, angry, hurt, etc. There are things that may exist before the communication began and may have nothing to do with either person or the content of the discussion. Yet, these things can set the stage for a readiness to have their heart at war or at peace with the other person. In addition, the nature of the present communication could bring up things reminiscent of a more hurtful past with that person or someone else.

*Chapter 14*

# Example of Unintentional Destruction of a Person's Spirit

Let us consider a story that illustrates an example of a person's spirit being destroyed by another. In this example, the "doer" is not aware of the effects that are taking place on the receiver. And, to some extent, the receiver is not fully aware of the fact that they are being destroyed in that moment, yet they can feel that something is amiss.

This story centers around an adult woman who was diagnosed with brain cancer. She endured brain surgery, chemotherapy, and a lengthy time in the hospital. She had more worries than joy during that time in her life because she was a caregiver by nature. She devoted her entire life to giving to others and attending to their needs in every way that she could. She was an avid football lover and a devoted Ravens fan. That year, while she was in the hospital recovering from surgery, she watched the Ravens playoff football game from her hospital bed. She longed to be at home with her children and husband and she longed to be at that game. The excitement was mixed because it gave her a small joy to experience, hearing the cheers of fans in the hallway of the hospital, but she also had a strong awareness that she was missing out in the fun, and in life in that moment. The Ravens lost that game, not earning a spot in the Super Bowl, and her disappointment grew. Her father spoke to her on the phone that day and promised her that he would take her to the Super Bowl the next year under two conditions. First, if she made it out of the hospital, surviving the cancer; and second, if the Ravens earned a spot in the Super Bowl championship game.

As the next year unfolded, she was on the path of recovery. She came home healthy, her hair started to grow back slowly, and she reclaimed her identity as a wife and as a mother. The next football season started and her excitement grew as the Ravens did very well, so well in fact that they earned their spot in the 2013 Super Bowl. She reflected on the past year, healing both physically and emotionally day by day. The anticipation grew as the football season progressed. Not only did she have the hope of a good season for the Ravens, but she also had the hope that she could actually attend the championship game in person with her favorite team. To her, this would have made up for the disappointing play off game the previous year in the hospital bed.

Several weeks before the final play off game to decide the Super Bowl teams, her guilt was growing that perhaps it was too much to ask of her father; that he may not be able to afford to take her to the Super Bowl. She felt stuck because she longed for it so much in the past year. She finally felt a small sense of being rewarded for enduring so much, yet it would have been hard for her to accept her father's gift. As the Ravens won and it was clear that they were going to the Super Bowl, she called her father to share in her excitement. He was reluctant and hesitant on the phone regarding fulfilling his promise. Her fears of guilt were validated as he shared his concern that it would be unfair to her other adult siblings and that perhaps he could find a way to pay for half of her ticket to go there and to pay for half of another ticket for one of her siblings to go with her.

She was crushed, left feeling deflated, devalued, and dismissed once again in her life. She did not want to seem ungrateful, so she accepted his offer and regained a smaller portion of her excitement. She picked a sibling to go with her and they started the planning process. As the next week unfolded, her father's position on the matter worsened as he proclaimed that he could not afford to pay for any portion of her ticket nor her sister's, and that he was sorry. It was too much to spend in his opinion and too much possible discord in the rest of the family if one or two were to go and not the rest. He pulled out and chose to not honor his promise.

This, unfortunately, was quite a hurtful moment in her life. To her, it ranked right up their with the stress and horror of her initial brain cancer diagnosis. She was disappointed again and was left to pick up the pieces by herself. She did not wish to upset her family in any way and did not want to appear as if she was "owed" anything. Yet, she recognized that she was the one diagnosed with brain cancer, she was the one who had surgery and chemo therapy, she was the one who spent months in treatment, and she was the one who was promised a Ravens Super Bowl ticket if she made it through this alive. It was not her sisters, her brother, nor anyone else. Why did *they* have to be connected to this promise between a father and his adult daughter who had struggled to live? It was unfair and very hurtful.

This was not acknowledged or discussed in the family. She watched the Super Bowl from her TV at home that year, celebrated somewhat in the Ravens Super Bowl victory, but mostly felt nauseous and uneasy during the entire game. She was not able to be there even though she lived up to her end of the bargain and the Ravens lived up to their end of the bargain. However, her father did not live up to his end of the bargain because of money and what he believed to have been an unfair situation to his other adult children. In a discussion with me about this, she was able to see that despite her feelings of guilt that would have made it difficult to accept these tickets in any circumstance, that it was in fact "unfair" that she had cancer to begin with. She had spent all of that time in treatment, in hospitals, doctor's appointments, and had to wear hats in public until her hair grew back.

The dangerous component in this example of spirit destruction was that this plagued her far beyond the disappointment about not being able to attend the game. She grappled with intense internal struggles between feeling selfish and feeling hurt that promises were broken to spare the feelings of her other siblings. She felt guilty to even think of accepting a large gift like that, believing that her father could not afford such an expense. She felt guilt that it would seem unfair to her other adult siblings and she even felt guilt for having feelings of hurt and frustration that this special promise was broken. The guilt was instilled in her from early childhood and had plagued her in her adult life, guiding her to mostly make decisions based out of guilt and the avoidance of guilt. She had become co-dependent in most of her relationships with others, enabling of their unhealthy patterns of behavior, and too tolerant of her feelings of hurt and isolation from others. She is a giver and a doer for others, asking for very little in return.

The reason why it was so important for this Super Bowl game ticket to have happened was that it was supposed to be a symbolic way to unlock and break these unhealthy patterns in her life. She was a loving and dedicated wife and mother. She got diagnosed with cancer, endured the treatment, survived, and healed. In the process, she allowed the hope of a future Ravens Super Bowl game to give her motivation and joy. It finally came true! Something that she desired, something that she needed, something that she did not even ask for but was offered to her and promised, had actually come true. She worked so hard to finally accept this joy but then it was taken away. The short circuit in this scenario was money and other people's potential feelings. Sadly, it had happened to her again, and it left her feeling hurt, lost, lonely, and confused. Though it is valid to be considerate and mindful of the expensive cost of an experience like this, there are times in which money only represents paper and ink.

On a cosmic and energetic level, we do not know the role that the hope of attending a Super Bowl game with her favorite team played in her healing and treatment. It is possible that it kept her alive, it is possible that it changed her biochemistry and allowed her body to be more receptive to medical treatment, and it is possible that it cut down on her medication costs and doctor visits. It is even possible that her strong feelings about this event helped to influence circumstances in the universe to allow this to happen. Perhaps she even aided in the manifestation of this win for the Ravens? There is no way of knowing this. However, it is clear that one cannot put a dollar figure on this experience and the powerful magnitude in which everything unfolded for her in her life since the cancer diagnosis.

*Chapter 15*

# How to Counteract and Transform Negative Energy

In this section, I hope to illustrate an example of how to cope with, shift, and release intense negative energy that has caused great distress and trauma. The following is just one example during the course of my work with a woman in her late 50s. She has decided that it would be meaningful to share part of her story. It is her hope that others could perhaps benefit from the journey of her experience and the journey of her healing. With respect to her privacy, we will refer to her as "Mary."

Mary was referred to me by her primary care physician due to concerns about her symptoms of depression, anxiety, and distress. He felt that it would be important to supplement the medicinal treatment of these symptoms with a talking therapy. Research shows psychotropic medication to be much more effective when used in conjunction with supportive psychotherapy. I will never forget the first time I met Mary. She came into my office with such a polite, tender, and pleasant smile and comforting energy. Mary shared that she was married to her husband for over 35 years, had three adult children, and a few grandchildren at the time. She was the type of woman you may associate with June Cleaver (from the Leave it to

Beaver TV show in the late 1950s) or perhaps a blend of Betty Crocker and Martha Stewart. I intend to use these references in a positive way, namely, that she was the type of person you could connect with instantly. She was approaching her 58th birthday and reported feeling overwhelmed, tearful, and anxious most of the time throughout the day.

As we began to get acquainted, she shared that she had been battling depression and anxiety for most of her life and believed it to stem back to an experience in early adolescence in which she was sexually molested. In a short moment she was in tears and she said that she wanted the man who did this to her "to get out of my life, out of my head, out of my marriage, and out of my bed." It became very clear that what happened to her, about 45 years before, was carried with her every day since. There was no escaping, no relief, and there was a justifiable sense that it was unfair that "he" still had "power" over her.

As our time together progressed, we learned that there were many things from her past that had plagued her, thus culminating in an overall feeling of despair and hopelessness. She was a remarkable and strong person who was loving and dedicated to her family and to others. She was present as a wife, as a mother, as a grandmother, and as an active church member. On the surface there was no evidence that she ever felt anything but joy. However, the emotional scar from the past ran very deep within her: a silent burden to bear.

We began to explore more about her life, her family of origin, her fundamentalist Christian upbringing, and her current beliefs about Religion, Spirituality, and God. We discovered that she was plagued with feelings of self-doubt, the fear of doing something "wrong," the search for finding the "right" answer in life, and the communication blocks between her and her husband. She had been married for about 38 years to a loving man who was devoted to her, supportive, and who was as kind and gentle as she. Yet, they both had difficulty expressing their feelings, sharing their love for each other, and Mary sometimes felt that there was an invisible barrier between them emotionally and physically.

We soon began to sense strong energy, that this journey could be healing, cathartic, and helpful to her, to myself, to her family, and perhaps for others as well. We spent many hours together learning about what she thought, how she felt, and how she experienced the world around her. She was a very spiritual person and found great comfort in her faith and in the foundations and principles of living a life in honor of God. We knew that our work would eventually need to include recounting the details of what happened as a child, and possibly re-experiencing the trauma associated with it.

Mary began to prepare herself for what we knew would be an

extremely difficult, time consuming, and disruptive process. We took our time, operating in as much comfort as we could provide her, giving her the freedom to decide the pace and the direction of our exploration. We monitored her symptoms of anxiety and depression very closely and worked on ways to start to regain control of her body and psychological responses to discussing this trauma. We also developed an idea to help ground and comfort her during the times in between our appointments in which the anxiety skyrocketed.

During our discussion about the events and circumstances regarding what happened during the sexual abuse, we discovered that one of the most difficult things about the experience was that it occurred during a church outreach activity. We needed to neutralize and transform the negative energy of this paradox. Namely, enduring a horrible experience while being engaged in something that is supposed to be rejuvenating and protective. One way to do that would be to use the positive part of the paradox to aid in healing. Mary remembered that she still had the small pocket bible that she carried with her as a child and even on the very day of the abuse. I asked her to bring it in so that we could look at it together, to notice the energy of what it felt like to hold it again, and to see if we could use it to help us in our journey. She brought in the bible for the next appointment and our work catapulted to the next level.

It came to me in flash that perhaps she could write down thoughts, notes, and questions about what happened to her in between our appointments with the goal in mind of being able to "download" them. The hope was that this would allow thoughts to be released from her mind and taken out of her body; she experienced anxiety in a psychological and physiological way. During our discussion about this, it also occurred to me that perhaps keeping these small notes in the pages of her childhood bible may help her to feel safe and comforted, that God will keep them for her so she did not have to. Mary began this exercise and noticed a shift in her feeling state each time she had an upsetting thought or question. She found it very helpful to write these things on paper, to get them out of her mind, and to store them safely away in that bible.

The next portion of our work together was to explore each note, the meaning and reaction to them, and then to compare them to the scripture written on each page of the bible where she "randomly" placed the note. In a remarkable and unexpected way, we noticed an amazing parallel between the thoughts and feelings in each note and the messages within the scripture. Mary began to feel that this process was being guided by God and that there was nothing left to "randomness." We spent many appointments in this phase of our work and it proved to be helpful on a healing level, an energetic level, and on a spiritual level. However, we realized that there was much more work to do.

There were two themes that emerged regarding Mary's block in understanding how to make sense out of what happened to her, why this happened, and how to free herself from her inner imprisonment of guilt and shame. We realized that one reason why she felt "stuck" for all of these years was because she never told anyone about what happened, no one except for her husband many years later. Even in that discussion, she kept the information brief and vague. As mentioned, Mary grew up in a very conservative fundamental Christian home and there were very clear expectations as to how she was to behave, what was acceptable/unacceptable, how to interact with adults, and what to fear and conform to. Even as an adult, she found it difficult to share a family wedding picture with her mother back home who was suffering from dementia. She was anxious about her mother's reaction because the picture was an image of Mary dancing and enjoying herself at the wedding. In her hometown, dancing was viewed as an evil ploy from the devil. So, when she became of victim of this horrific act of betrayal by a man in the neighborhood, Mary felt paralyzed during that moment and after. She was taught to respect her elders, to do what she was told, and to not say upsetting things about other people. Sadly, her voice was taken from her.

Mary kept her silence in isolation from her family of origin. Another reason why Mary felt stuck for all of those years was because this occurred during a community outreach activity for the church; it was confusing and unbearable. Mary was asked to go door to door in the neighborhood to pass out pamphlets about an upcoming church activity. She was doing her service as a responsible member of the church, community, and of her family, but she was betrayed. A man asked her to come into his home and began to molest her. Years later, her older brother eventually became the pastor of that very church in which the family was active participants. We began to realize that perhaps there was a way to reconcile with the hurt and confusion resulting from not being able to speak to her family to get love and support, as well as, a chance to heal with the church. Though she remained active in church, since suffering at the hands of her abuser she never quite felt the guidance and protection from her faith that she once had in her youth. She struggled with feeling let down by church and by God because this evil happened to her.

We decided that our work would then shift to an extreme focus on how to resolve these inner conflicts. We made the decision that she could write a series of two letters with the belief that describing what happened to her could help her to regain some sense of control, comfort, and re-connection with her family and God. One letter was to her elderly mother and the other was to her older brother. We did not know if these letters would ever be sent, but we believed that there was something powerful in the symbolic energy of writing them. The first letter was written to her mother and I feel it necessary to share what was written here.

*Dear Mom,*

*I feel a sense of urgency in the need to write to you. I don't know that you will see this in your lifetime that remains here on earth. Every time I think of you, which is often, or pick up the phone to call you, I am reminded that one day soon will be your last. I need you to know that I love you. I would like to hear you say that you love me even though I already know you do. I understand the culture you lived and were raised in was not a touching and expressive culture; I don't really know about your life growing up. It must have been terribly hard financially - that Grandpa and Grandma must have worked very hard to care for you and your brothers and sisters. It must have been equally as difficult for you. I also recognize that you and Dad worked very hard to care for me and the other kids. You must have made many sacrifices. I appreciate that you were always physically present. I fear that I needed more than that physical presence; I needed your emotional presence as well. I never felt like I could approach you with things that were on my mind, or experiences I was having. I needed to be taken into your heart.*

*Do you remember the time when I was about 10 years old, you let me wear your only wristwatch outside, and I lost it? I was so afraid to tell you that I wrote you a note - I knew that I had to confess my sin. You never said anything about it. I needed acknowledgment of some kind. I wanted to hear that you would miss the watch, but that it was just a watch, and that you love me anyway. I never felt like I knew where I stood in your heart.*

*There is one more thing that I need to tell you about - a time I was so frightened and could not tell you or anyone what had happened to me and what I was thinking and feeling. I've spent a lifetime trying to bury it. Sometimes that seemed to work, but it didn't really. So, some of the details seem to be gone. When I was in the 6th or 7th grade, well into physically maturing, some friends and I met the pastor in town to pass out pamphlets for the revival. I think it was summer because it was hot. We split up so we could canvas the whole town. Armed with fliers, we went knocking on doors to invite people. In some cases I knew the kids in the house, but in many, I did not know the person or they weren't home.*

*I had one horrible experience that day. It was in a house close to the main street and not far from the church. I had no idea who lived there and what awaited me. I walked up to the house and knocked on the screen door - I think there was a small screened in porch. I could see the door into the house was open. There was no answer. I knocked again and waited. I started to put the pamphlet in the door to leave and then heard a muffled "who's there?" I don't recall if I said my name, but I called out that I just wanted to leave a pamphlet. He then said, "come in." I felt compelled to go inside. As I stepped through the doorway into the house, I saw an older man sitting upright on what I think was a bed up against one wall.*

*He was older, unshaven, dressed in an undershirt and overalls. His hair was uncombed and gray. His speech was not clear. I knew I must have awakened him from a nap and I felt bad that I had disturbed him.*

*I had a bad feeling but didn't know why. So I began to explain why I was there-I told him about the revival and offered him the pamphlet. He couldn't reach it as I held it out; I'm not sure if he asked me to come closer, of if I was just accommodating his needs. So I stepped closer. He wanted to talk about the pamphlet. I stepped closer and he pulled me to sit on his thigh. Before long, he had one arm around my shoulders and the other creeping up my leg. Before much longer, his mouth was on my breast, one hand fondling the other breast and his fingers inside me, between my legs, in my vagina. I did not know what was going on and only wanted it to end-to be out of there. I don't know how long it took for him t o get what he needed. He released me. I straightened myself and he gave me a quarter so I could "get something cold to drink."*

*I don't really remember anything more about that day, except going to the dairy queen and getting a milk shake. I think I even told you later about an older man that gave me money for a drink. I was afraid to tell you the rest. I didn't know what had happened, or that there were people in the world who could do such things. So I buried it, hoping it would go away. Shortly after marrying Sam, it came back to me in the midst of lovemaking. I still didn't understand it, but knew that it was unfair for me to not tell Sam. So I gave him a brief description, still burying details. That seemed to help for a while. In the years since, it continues to enter my living and Sam's. I am working now to truly deal with this and with our relationship, and my relationship to others. It is important to me to share this with you. I don't know right now that I will actually send this to you while you're living. There are other things in my life that I wish I could have shared with you, many good things, or at least things that make me feel happy or proud. My behavior did not always fit the good behavior outline-the parties, fashion shows, dancing, even stuff with the kids. I don't want to imply that you are responsible for where I am in my life. I made adult choices along the way. You taught me so many good things. I only wish to hear the words "I love you Mary" and to feel the emotion in a hug, and to say to you "I love you mom" and to hug you.*

*Your loving and needful daughter,*

*Mary*

Needless to say, this was a difficult letter for her to write and for her to read out loud to me. She was brave, courageous, strong, and in this act, began to regain some sense of control in her life. As we worked through the reactions to this exercise, she eventually became ready to write the second letter to her brother the pastor. I felt as strong desire to help her to feel comforted, supported, and protected during this process, much like during the time when she wrote notes and placed them into her childhood bible. I asked her if she felt that it would be better for her to write the next letter in the safety of my office, with me present, and with the focus and energy of healing. She decided that it would be helpful and we began the next phase of her writing. We determined that it would be helpful for me to write about my own thoughts and experiences during our work so that we could see if there were connections like we found between her notes and in the Bible scripture. What followed was an amazing experience for both of us. I will now share the next letter that Mary wrote to her brother, and then the notes that I wrote in tandem with her while she was in my office.

*Dear Peter,*

*You will find a quarter attached to this page. This is a special letter for me. I chose you to receive it because I think you will understand and perhaps use some little piece of my experience in your ministry to others. I am also looking for some peace for myself - peace that comes from sharing with you.*

*When mom came ill with dementia a few years ago, I slipped over the edge into a depression I had been fighting for years. I found help through the guidance of a wonderful therapist, Greg, who has shared this journey with me. I know God is working through him to help me. I have a story to tell you that I hope can help someone else. I was never able to tell mom and dad; I want and need to tell you, to achieve a level of family intimacy, trust, and love that I feel has escaped me over the years.*

*When I was a young teen, I was helping hand out fliers announcing a gospel meeting at the church. My friends and I met at the church and were assigned different areas of town to knock on doors and invite people to come. It was a warm afternoon. As you remember, where we grew up was a safe small town USA. I don't know about the others, but I was alone. I only remember one house that I went to that day. It was just north of Main Street and within 1 or 2 blocks of church. It was a bit of a shanty, with a screened in front porch. I walked up the 1 or 2 steps and knocked on the wooden frame of the screen door, flier in hand.*

*There was an almost inaudible response of "come in." I opened the screen and crossed the porch to the front door. There was an older man sitting on the bed dressed in undershirt and overalls. I recited my line telling him about the revival and inviting him to come. I held out the flier but he couldn't reach it sitting on the bed. I stepped closer. He took my hand and pulled me onto his lap. He held me there and moved me around rubbing against his penis. He fondled me in private areas. He suckled my child breast. Back then all that I knew was feeling frightened. But now, I realized that he sexually assaulted me - just short of rape. He finally released me and handed me a quarter so I could get something cold to drink. I knew that what he did was wrong. I thought that I must also have done something wrong. I didn't know people behaved like that. I met evil face to face. I could find no way to tell anyone.*

*I have carried feelings of guilt of contamination with me all of my life. That man has crept into my waking thoughts and into my dreams. He has been in my head and my relationships even though I tried desperately to forget all of it. Sam has done what he could to help me with this over the years. With Greg's help and God's guidance, I'm beginning to truly heal. We happened upon a technique that I'm sure God led us on. Early in our sessions we discovered that I had repeating internal questions and thoughts. Greg urged me to write them down as they occurred and to put them in a "safe place" so then I could remove them from my mind until we talked. The safe place I chose was a child's bible that contained the New Testament and Psalms and Proverbs that our neighbor gave me when I was about 10. When a question came to me, I randomly stuck the note in that Bible.*

*I did this over the course of many weeks. Then Greg and I began to read the questions one at a time. We also read the pages of the Bible the questions were filed in. Then we talked about it. Without fail, there was something contained in the scripture that applied to my questions; they were like answers directly from God. I am certain God led me. The process brought me great comfort and reassurance that God had not abandoned me and this horrible experience could somehow be put to good use. This is where I ask for your help. The quarter is representative of the quarter the man gave me that made me feel "bought" all of these years. It should be put to good use, God's use.*

*I trust you as my brother and as a minister of God to make a good decision. Perhaps this quarter can simply be placed as a contribution in the plate and be blessed for God's work here on earth. Or perhaps there is someone you have counseled, or one day will counsel, that would benefit from my story. God waited patiently for me to turn to him and the gift of scripture.*

*I said at the beginning of this letter that I was not able to share this experience with mom or dad. I was so afraid that I had done something wrong. I know now that I didn't do anything wrong. I was a child that didn't know such things happened and shame kept me afar from family, from friendships, and in a dark place. God will lead both you and me to something good. I want something good to come from this. I am watching, waiting, and praying.*

*Mary*

As mentioned, Mary wrote this specific letter only while in my office and while I wrote in tandem with her. Below is the account of my experience of her and our time together while she wrote about her own story.

First Writing

Mary has given me the privilege of journaling with her in her efforts to battle depression and anxiety. In our beginning discussions, it was discovered that she had endured a traumatic experience in her early teens in which a neighborhood man sexually molested her while she was engaged in a church outreach project. This had caused considerable distress and it was exacerbated by the extra stress of feeling guilt and feeling loneliness as she had no one to turn to. The pain ran deep and it was carried with her for over 40 years. It factored into her marriage and in her bed, and it came into my office with her.

During the course of our work together, we learned about who Mary was and is. In her heart she is a kind, compassionate, loving, creative, hard working woman who is devoted to her husband, her family, her religion, and God. However, her shell was fragile and it was weakened by self-doubt, fear, issues with authority figures, and a confusion about her direction, meaning, and purpose.

We also learned that there was the presence of a higher power with us in our emotional travels. We bridged gaps and made connections that neither of us could have predicted. We found some levels of understanding about different things Mary was experiencing that could not be put into tangible terms. We also generated ideas that offered her excitement, empowerment, and emotional freedom that seemed to have been softly whispered into our souls. Yet, despite all of these successes, small and distant signals of pain still lingered and we decided that it was important to go further beyond our discussions. For example, the writing that was done with Bible scripture, the releasing of the 1965 quarter that was given to her by this hurtful man, and the way she was able to be supportive of her daughter-in-law during her own experience of sexual abuse. At this point we decided that it was time to write to the church where this all began, back to genesis.

Second Writing

It is our expectation that writing this letter will allow Mary to release this pain, to separate her identity from the actions of this man, to find peace with God, to share and inspire those in this community, and to achieve emotional support from her family of origin that had been so unavailable to her in the past. As I write this section of my thoughts, Mary has begun to write section two of her letter to her brother Peter, the section in which I have called the "factual details" and the section in which she has called "the body."

I notice the symbolism of "the body"- presented as part of a complete formal letter, yet also representing her actual physical body and how intertwined her literal experiences are with how she now sees herself. She is so strong and so courageous right now despite the emotional vulnerability deep within. She is operating from a very spiritual place and she is gaining power and control in this very moment.

With each painful word that is written, she is finding herself closer to relief and closer to God. It seems that the key to her detachment from what happened to her rests in the distinct shift in her belief that it was an unfortunate and evil act that happened to her and <u>not</u> an event that defined or defines the core essence of who she is. This shift will allow her to recall the details of what happened without stirring up her emotions, leaving her victim to the trauma over and over again. She will take away this man's power and cast him out of her life, giving him to God, much like God has cast out Satan.

## Third Writing

Today, Mary has described her recent visit to see her mother in her childhood hometown. She shared how she spent time caring for her mother, reconnecting with her siblings, and her experience in church - at <u>the</u> church, the church that her father literally built, the church with the Fundamental Christian doctrine, the church that asked her to go door to door on a mission, the church that stands within eye sight, or a stone's throw as I would like to say, from the home of the man who violated her body and stole her trust. This is the church where her brother is now pastor and where she may send the letter in hopes of releasing the pain caused so many years ago.

When I mentioned that I hoped that she was proud of herself - for her courage and positive energy - she stated that she was "saving pride, saving pride for another time, kind of filing it away for later." I stated that there was a different peace in this statement for Mary – it was not influenced by the usual self-doubt, feeling undeserving, or unworthy, this time it was an acknowledgment that great steps were being made and that, as a result of her patience and hard work, she would soon be able to celebrate freedom from the hold the past experiences had on her. She could sense that she is on the verge of a powerful shift and that she was in the presence of something Godly and life sustaining.

Mary will likely return for another trip in the near future. I am wondering if that trip will be the opportunity to send/give the letter back to church, or if already done by that time, if that trip will allow her to leave all of the pain back at the source where it all began, at ground zero, at the place that shook her from her foundation and changed her life.

Fourth Writing

In this writing, I am inspired to contemplate two intertwining components. The first being what I will call her growing strength and presence and the second being a possible higher calling for helping others to heal. I have found myself thinking about Mary a bit more frequently in between recent appointments. There seems to be a blend of her courage, strength, and spiritual presence that whispers in my ear. It is like healing has lifted a cloud or fog or opaque shadow around her that once masked who she was. She appears to be brighter, more independent, and more solid. Within this momentum, my thoughts migrate to where this journey will take her. What role does God want her to fulfill? Yet, this thought also scares me and I want to proceed cautiously because I do not wish for her to feel obligated or burdened-essentially replaying old roles and themes with authority figures.

Mary appears to me in my thoughts as a beacon of strength and light. There are so many that could benefit from her wisdom, perspective, and resiliency. I am reminded about her ability to find love and comfort with God in spite of evil being done to her in the presence of the church. I see other women in my practice with traumatic backgrounds that have become shattered, fragile, and broken. Yet, I see courage and strength in them as well. Mary is magnifying it each day and the parts of her that would conceal and consume her are starting to fade. How does one continue his/her path and give to others at the same time? Perhaps in order to continue to walk our path, we <u>must</u> give to others?

Fifth Writing

During our healing journey, Mary had the opportunity to be present for her daughter-in-law, Ally, during a rough time in which Ally confronted her own step-father about being sexually abused by him. This was a delicate time for Mary because it was saddening that Ally had been treated in this way, it was emotionally destabilizing because it brought her past to the surface more, and yet it was cathartic because Mary was able to be present for Ally in a way that no one was able to do for Mary herself. She described today that the trial of Ally's stepfather was postponed (because the defense attorney could not ethically represent him) and that it may be rescheduled for around the time that Mary and Sam would be visiting.

The purpose of that trip was to support Ally in a body sculpting fitness competition. It is amazing how people find ways to cope with trauma. Sometimes people physically retreat after a sexual abuse and experience great discomfort with the body, yet other times some people can go through a metamorphosis and showcase it, as if it were a rebirth or baptism. In describing this, and other current anxiety, it is extremely noticeable how much Mary has grown and how strong she has become. It feels like our goal of emotionally detaching from what happened to her is being reached. While there is certainly pain still present, the power and effect it once had continues to diminish. Mary is a fierce warrior who fights with heart, compassion, purity, and goodness and not with anger, vengeance, or hate. Her weapons are much more powerful and her success is much more secured.

Sixth Writing

Mary is beginning the final section of her writing, the section we are calling the summary-where she will be putting together the plan and hope for how she will heal and the plan and hope in sharing this with her brother Peter. After each writing session, I notice what appears to be a greater peace and stillness within her. It also looks as if she has reversed aging about 5 years. Perhaps the burden that she has carried with her, like an emotional scarlet letter, is lifting? I find myself excitedly waiting to hear what Mary has written and I sense that it will offer her and countless other people so much healing.

I believe that the greatest gift or value of how she will harness this energy shift will not be through examples of strength, courage, and resiliency, but through the gift of hope and faith. This may serve as an example that things can get better and that we do have the ability to influence and integrate our internal and external worlds. Also, that faith in a higher power, or a belief system that there are greater and far more complex things at work in the universe, can helps us to operate outside of what we think or see in front of us.

I recently saw the movie Avatar and was pleasantly struck by the beautiful spirituality portrayed and strong parallels to Native American culture. It illustrated how connected each living thing is to one another and to nature. That there is constant communication and interaction, much more than with the billions of neurons communicating and sending and receiving messages in the human body. What a nice reminder that there is a purpose and meaning in all things and how important it is to take the time to listen for and appreciate the message and signals we encounter each moment of our lives. We get too lost and travel too far off course at times. It looks like Mary is finding her way back to her core, to exist in unison with her spirituality and free herself from the invisible prison and chains of what happened to her so many years ago.

## Seventh Writing

During our last appointment, Mary decided to re-read the letter she wrote to her mother describing what happened to her. She wrote it just over 2 years ago and it remains a powerful example of her courage, strength, and continued awareness of the emotional impact of what she experienced. As she writes in this very moment, she is leaning forward in her chair in a different way than in the recent past. It is as if she is writing with more intention/pro-activity, sprinting to the finish line. This speaks to me as an act of anticipation of the release she hopes to feel after she is done writing, and not a matter of anxious energy. Mary is growing more proficient with her self-awareness, recognizing the difference between intuition and anxiety, and she is finding the courage to follow her gut instincts. She continues to experience inner paradoxes as she recognizes areas of progress, yet she is plagued by whispers of self-doubt and negative self-evaluation. She is recognizing that it is time to let go of these old patterns. We have strong hope. (End of journal writing)

As a summary to this chapter on how to counteract and transform negative energy, I would like to describe a little more about what happened next for Mary. In the work that followed, Mary remained unsure as to what to do with these letters. Though she still liked the idea of sending the letter that she wrote to her brother, there was something that held her back. We discovered a missing key component in her ability to make a decision was that we had not included her husband Sam in the healing process. We began to set up a series of meetings with Mary, Sam, and me so that we could discover the next step together.

After some time, it became clearer to us that there needed to be a physical release in some way. We thought it best to plan a "releasing ceremony" in which she and Sam would read the letter together, say what they wished, and then burn it. We thought that it would be important to watch the physical form of the letter disintegrate into the atmosphere. We spent time trying to structure how to do this, the when and the where. They both reported feeling an immense sense of relief and regaining control over their lives. However, there was still one small missing component, namely, the quarter. The quarter was a symbolic representation of feeling "bought," feeling ashamed, and feeling silenced.

In another epiphany, we decided to plan a "destruction ceremony" in which the quarter would be smashed and cast away into the pasture. Though I was not present for that experience, it was amazing to hear the story of how Sam prepared a steel plate to sit the quarter on top, heating it with a blow torch, and then Mary smashing the quarter with a heavy sledgehammer. Can you image June Cleaver with a sledgehammer? They both described the power of the clashing sound of metal against metal, as well as, the power of the feeling the vibration in the handle. They felt the power of a strong energy shift and they were able to release so much internal negative energy, transforming from inside their body and soul and being redirected right into that tiny coin. It was a form of transferring the disrupted energy within them into a physical item. After that experience, they felt better equipped to truly move past this trauma and to reforge a new life together free from the restriction and weight of the past.

# Chapter 16

# What to Pay Attention To and How to Fix an Energy Short Circuit

This next scenario represents a very embarrassing and difficult story to tell regarding what I believe was a large error on my part as a parent. Some people who read this may connect with the experience of managing children in a store when they are insisting that you buy them something. It can be an overwhelming and frustrating experience. I am not sure, however, if you will agree with what I perceive as my error in the following example.

On one sunny but chilly day in the early part of the spring, we decided as a family to take a trip to a small old town main street in which my wife and I spent much of our time together while dating before marriage and children. It was a quaint little town with small mom and pop type shops and we were excited to show the kids where their mommy and daddy used to sit on a rock, talk, and watch people walk by. My wife also wished to take the kids into a small antique shop where there was a vendor that sold Legos (plastic building blocks). They had advertised a special in which you could fill a small container of assorted Legos for $5 each. As we made our way into the store and started collecting containers and Lego pieces, my youngest daughter, then 3 ½ years old, saw another showcase with various Lego figures. Inside of that case was a small section of white Lego horses used in knight sets that Lego produced. She asked to see the horse, which had no price tag on it, and I decided that there would be no harm in taking a closer look.

As we asked for assistance from one of the helpers in the antique store, we realized that the owner of this booth was not present. Since there was no price tag on this container of horses, the helper suggested a price of $4. We allowed our daughter to hold the horse for a while as we collected more Legos and walked around the store, taking our time to make a decision; we had already filled up three buckets with assorted Legos for each of the kids. My dilemma grew stronger as I was acutely aware of feeling torn between the notion of getting her this very coveted horse versus counter acting the pattern of our children getting things from the stores we walk into during weekends. This dilemma was beyond the $4 cost, it was the principle of instilling more patience within the kids, more awareness and gratitude for what they have, how much things cost, how difficult it is to make money, etc. I try to be mindful about working with my children in learning to delay gratification and to not overindulge.

In addition, it seemed to me that $4 was a tad high of a price to pay for a single Lego horse, it seemed worth more like $2 to me and we were not even sure if the $4 was the correct price since the owner was not there and the helper was just guessing. My wife and I discussed it for a couple of moments and asked the helper if the store would be willing to sell this for the $2 price we were comfortable with. He declined and we decided not to buy the horse. As I was paying for the rest of the things at the front register, my wife explained our decision to my daughter, who took it very well. She did not cry, yell, demand it, or throw a tantrum. She had a sad face, hugged her mommy, and put her head down on her mommy's shoulder. The pain of this image haunts me even as I write this in this very moment. It is hard to fight back my own tears because of her little broken spirit in that moment.

It became very apparent to me that this decision was a mistake. I was stuck and I did not know what to do. We left the store shortly after and I mentioned to my wife that I needed to go back to this store and fix this mistake. She reassured me that our daughter was okay with our decision, that she did not <u>need</u> to have the horse, and that it would be okay to let this bad feeling go. Sadly, I could not let it go and I wrestled with this for the next hour or so that we were visiting the main street shops. I could tell that something was not right and the guilt plagued me. I tried to rationalize my decision with the logic of what my wife suggested and how she was likely correct in her opinion. However, I was thinking about the significance of the horse and that interaction for my daughter. Her older sister has loved horses since early toddler-hood and shared that passion with our youngest. Our, youngest, Leah for easier reference, adores her older sister Abigail and they have developed a very special bond in their short time together. Leah has also developed her own love and passion for zebras in addition to her horse love from her older sister, and Lego love from her older brother Jake, our middle child. I was captivated by how she was drawn right to this particular horse with the yellow saddle in an entire store full of other items. She had walked around the store with the horse in one hand, and her daddy's hand in the other. She went on a special adventure to explore the store and she explained that the horse was guiding us on a tour.

While keeping this close to my heart, I became horrified of what I determined was a catastrophic mistake in not bringing this horse home with us. My self frustration and obsession continued into late into the evening. My wife tried very hard to help steer me in another direction, she gave me a wonderful option of searching on the internet to find used sets of Lego horses and to give Leah the option of picking out something else. We found several, in fact, the sets were fairly priced and included 5-8 of the Lego horses. This was a solid plan, and I am sure that Leah would have been happy to receive any of them. I thought about this until the early hours of the next morning, and then it occurred to me. There was only one fix. There was something very important about driving the hour or so distance each way, back to the same store, back to the same horse, to bring it home with us and to find the balance that was disrupted within my decision the day before. I do not believe that Leah experienced this trauma consciously in the same way that I did, but I do believe that this subtle trauma affected her nonetheless.

This decision was certainly extreme, excessive, and did not make any logical or even financial sense. Yet, it came to me in a flood of an epiphany, it quite simply had to be done. I had to ignore logic and reason and allow this to be guided by something more important and more powerful than my initial thoughts. So, that is exactly what we did. Leah, myself, and her granddad took the long trip back to the store, we found the horse that she was forced to leave behind and even the same helper from the day before. I felt so much better the closer we got to the store, and when she finally had the same horse back in her hands. The helper informed me that he was able to speak to the owner of the booth and the price was in fact $5 for the Lego horse. This did not matter to me, I just needed to right this wrong. As we drove home, Leah fell asleep in the car holding her horse, which she named "Step Step." She was exhausted because of the three flights of steps her little legs had to travel to get her back to him and back into her delicate fingers. The story does not end there, below is what I wrote to her and read that evening for her bedtime story:


## Step-Step the Lego Horse

Once upon a time there was a beautiful white horse who always wore his favorite yellow saddle. He was a lonely horse because he lived in a display case at Taylor's Antique store in Ellicott City. He was happiest when people would walk by to look at the things in the store. Sometimes little kids would come up to his case and look at the cool items around him. He was excited because he loved to see people and he thought that maybe they would play with him from time to time. It was dusty and cold in that store. There were some other toys around him but they did not move or talk like he did. In fact, he felt very lonely because he could never get people to hear his voice and understand him; it was very confusing to him.

He did not get to see many people because it was a long travel up many stairs to his section on the top floor. There were just too many steps to walk up for the little legs and feet of children. Also, since this was not a typical toy store and it carried many old items, he most spent his time trying to get his neighbors to play with him. He taught himself how to read and he realized that Lego figures do not actually move like him. They were plastic and they did not have souls of their own, they were used by children in their imaginary play. This horse, however, was very very different.

One day he heard quite a loud noise as a small group of children came up to visit. He could tell that there was one boy in the group because the boy wore very loud and clumpy boots as he stomped up the stairs. The boots were big and they were covered in dirt and a camouflage design. The horse got so excited as the children walked up the stairs to his section. But then he became sad and disappointed because he watched the children as they walked right by him. They filled up empty buckets with assorted Lego pieces from the display case in front of him. They spent many minutes there and he was confused because those Lego pieces were not special like him.

His sadness grew as he thought that they would never pay attention to him. But then, in one glorious moment, a tiny little princess turned around and noticed him. She saw him in a pile of other Lego horses but she knew he was special because he was the only one with a yellow saddle. She spoke to him and she could even hear his voice when he spoke back. This princess, who seemed to think that she was a "big girl" even though she was the smallest one in the group, wanted to save this horse from his lonely existence. She asked to hold him and the young man with the key to the display case gently put him in her hands. She walked around the store for the rest of their visit with the magical horse.

They introduced themselves to each to each other on their way down the long set of steps. She said that her name was Leah and he excitedly told her that his name was Step-Step. Step-step was so excited to have a new friend that he offered to take her on a tour of his home, the entire antique store, all four levels. She agreed and she took her daddy by the hand and walked both her daddy and Step-Step around the entire store. Leah wanted to rescue Step-Step and take him home with her. She talked to her parents and her mommy and daddy seemed to be unsure of bringing him home. He was only $4 but Leah's parents seemed stressed about the money they were spending on the other Legos for Leah and her brother and sister. The daddy seemed concerned about the money that was spent for lunch, the money that was going to be spent for dinner, and all of the other things that needed to be purchased that weekend. Sadly, Leah was told that she could not bring her new friend home.

Leah's daddy felt very upset about her disappointment for the rest of the day and night. He believed that he made a big mistake in not letting Leah bring home her new friend. Leah was not one to ask for much and she could find so much happiness in the smallest of things. Her daddy realized that he let his stress about money get in the way of what was a magical moment for Leah and her new friend. He decided that he had to fix this mistake the very next day and he drove back to the store with Leah, her older brother with the loud boots, and with her granddad. They drove almost one hour back to the store on a highway and many twisty, hilly, wooded roads. Leah was so excited to see her new friend right back in his display case and Step-Step could not believe his eyes.

He was heart broken from the previous night because he had never met anyone like Leah before. She connected with his spirit right away and he could tell that Leah would take very good care of him. He never knew a love like this before and he never felt that much pain before when he was put back in the display case. So naturally, he thought he was dreaming the next day when he heard the loud clumpy boots again and saw Leah's smiling face. He was so excited that he could not wait for the young man to find the right key to open the case. It seemed like an eternity before he could climb into Leah's hands again, though it must have only been a minute. They were finally reunited and Leah held him for the entire hour ride back home. Caressing him with a care, a nurturing, and a wisdom beyond her years as she fell asleep before arriving at Step-Steps new home.

Here is a picture of an exhausted Leah and her new friend Step-Step on their long Journey home after being reunited:

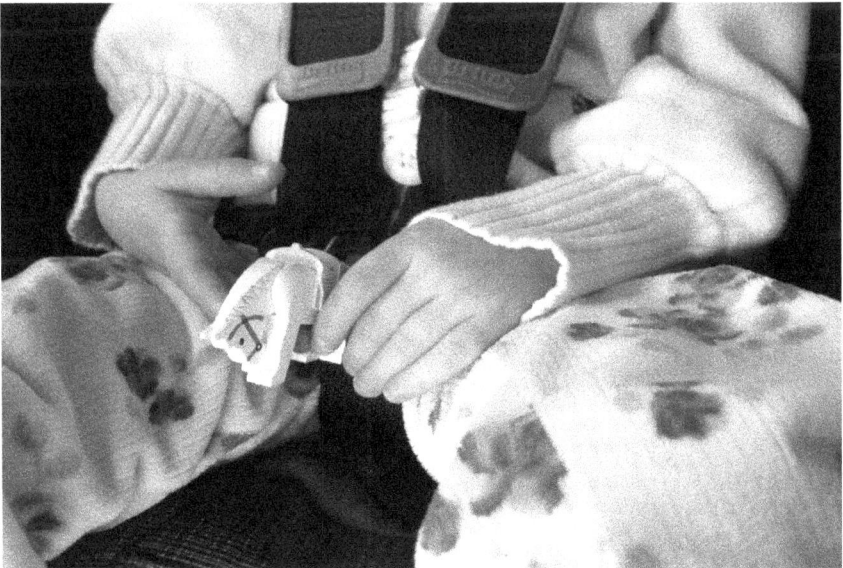

I believe that I found a resolution to fix the error that I made and have hopefully learned to not be short circuited in moments like this again in the future. I allowed my desire for a financial and consumer teaching lesson to overshadow the importance of that very special moment. I want to be sensitive to not destroying the spirit of my wife or my three children. I do not intend for this scenario to showcase me being a good father. Conversely, I believe it showcases the flaws in my character. I am not being too hard on myself because I can forgive this error. However, I do hope that this illustrates the importance of attentiveness in parenting or any interpersonal communication for that matter. It reminds me to stay focused and sharp and to accept my flaws and mistakes. More importantly, it reminds me to remain self aware, externally aware, and how to acknowledge and correct the things that I do that affect my loved ones in negative ways.

## Chapter 17

# How to Hone In on the Skill of Energy Theory

If we go back to a phrase used earlier in the book, "pay attention to everything but be affected by very little," we can start to put this to practical use. Many people have the first part mastered; paying attention to everything. If you ever feel yourself overwhelmed, stressed, or anxious, that cues you into the first part about "pay attention to everything." However, there is such a thing as paying too much attention to something as well. It is the second part, being affected by very little, that people tend to find far more difficult and complicated. Many of us who are givers, doers, helpers, and worriers often consider too much. We can become paralyzed with doubt, uncertainty, guilt, and frustration. This can become even more paralyzing if we are good at seeing more than one side to a situation, if we are flexible and open to things, or if we have difficulty making decisions.

Let us consider for a moment a classic scenario in which a young, newly engaged couple, decides to start planning their wedding. Often times, they are excited and unsure of the next steps but they begin their task with high hope that their wedding day will be one of their best memories in life together. They do not set out to fight, they do not view their marriage as a temporary arrangement, and they do not wish to spend more than they can afford. Inevitably, there are usually other family members on one or both sides that are enlisted to help or that volunteer themselves to help. As well intentioned as they are, this "help" tends to create tension for the soon to be bride or groom, or even tension between the bride and groom. It is quite symbolic actually because it is one of their first challenges as life partners. They are charged with the task of making decisions together as a unit and to sift through the challenge of factoring other people out of their relationship.

During this journey, the bride and groom will eventually migrate to the task of creating the guest list and organizing the seating arrangements. Here is where a break down and short circuit can occur as they try to balance what they want versus what their family may want. People often feel obligated and stuck to invite certain people from their past. They do not wish to offend or upset anyone, yet they may have strong desires for certain people not to attend their wedding, or they may even have a budget to consider and need to be highly selective regarding who should be invited. There are decisions to consider that involve factors such as who gets along in families; who has children and who does not; should children be invited; what will people do for childcare if children are not invited; is there alcohol served at the wedding; and who gets the ultimate say in the guest list. Many times if there are parents of the bride and groom that are involved, they have strong input that their own friends be added to the guest list. They may have a desire to share this special day with people who have meant something to them in the past, but they can get a little off track at times in this desire.

Using principles from this energy theory can be a freeing and simplifying agent in the midst of a dilemma such as this. The bride and groom can simply decide who they really want to share in their day, who they wish to witness their commitment to each other through vows to have a life together. They can monitor if they have any reactions to certain people on the guest list and if those reactions are unpleasant and could distract them or take away from their joyful and peaceful experience. If that is the case, then strong consideration should be put into whether or not to invite that person. However, if the conflict is between the bride or groom and his/her partner's family members, this becomes more complicated and requires a much more creative strategy. For the sake of illustrating this basic example, we will assume that to not be the case.

If the bride and groom monitor their reactions and determine a discomfort, then the internal simplicity and execution in their heart and mind would be as follows:

> "I simply wish to marry my best friend, there is no one in this world who makes me feel the way I do about myself when I am with him/her. I want to make this commitment to each other and share in this day with people who mean something very special to me and will support and enhance our choice to have this life together. I do not wish to be upset in this experience or to offend or upset anyone else. However, I am only willing to make decisions that work best for me and my partner and no one else. If these decisions do upset or offend other people, I will hold compassion in my heart for their feelings, but I will release myself from any guilt or obligation to fix or address anything for other people. This day will be a life changing day for me and my partner and we will only allow joy and love into this experience."

I believe that this mentality, this mantra, and this statement are powerful templates to guide decisions in a situation like this. I can appreciate that it will be difficult to implement and execute this philosophy, but the pay off is worth it and the cause is noble. I would recommend to couples who wish to take this philosophy, that this is where they stop. They adopt this philosophy, implement it, and have very little discussion with anyone else about the reactions and aftermath that follows from others. It can honestly be that simple. Sometimes, however, money becomes yet another short circuit if the person(s) contributing to the cost of the wedding have strong feelings and reactions themselves. Those financially supportive people may even go as far as to require having input in the wedding decisions as part of the agreement for their financial contribution.

If a couple feels stuck in this scenario because they do not have the financial means to plan the wedding as they would like, and they feel obligated to consider what the contributor wants, then I would suggest the following philosophy and dialogue:

> "We cannot express our gratitude enough for the financial support of our family. We believe that their financial support is not 'required' and that it is given with the intention of love and support. If, however, there are other emotional costs of accepting this financial support, then we will have to scale down our wedding plans, and operate in more of an affordable budget that works for us. This may mean that the vision for our wedding must change completely from what we intended and dreamed. Yet, the emotional cost and turmoil that comes attached to having this vision may not be worth it. Instead, the potentially drastic changes necessary to bring this experience back into our hands completely will be extremely worth it. Thank you again to our loved ones, we can accept your love, support, presence, and even financial support on this day, only on the condition that all of that can be given without complicated and negative costs."

Holidays are another opportunity for couples to have their relationship tested. In my line of work, I find this happens most frequently in how decisions are made regarding holiday visits, obligations, fun, family traditions, religious activities, etc. I have noticed over the years that the most upsetting time for people tends to be surrounding the holidays. There are likely a variety of things that factor into that, some of which include winter time with colder temperatures and less day light, financial burdens during the gift giving time of year, holidays and family time that cause us to look inward and reflect on life and circumstances, and possibly the end of a year and start of a New Year.

With that said, it is likely that many people can relate to the frustrations and stress of coordinating schedules, making decisions about whom to spend holiday time with, how to fit everything in, how to be fair to everyone, how to find some peaceful connection with loved ones, and hopefully how to find a little bit of relaxation away from work and day to day life struggles. We often hear people say things like, "well, we have to go to _____'s house, it's Thanksgiving and this is what we always do," or something like "We have to host _____ holiday this year, if we don't, then the family won't get together, and then it won't really be a good holiday." The list of examples of "shoulds" and "shouldn'ts" can go on and on. We also can easily imagine how upsetting it can be to a family if one part of a family or one family member decides to do something different one year. People either admire, understand, and respect that change, or they can react in judgment and criticism, feeling a betrayal that someone "broke the rules."

Let us consider for a moment the powerful energy shift in one individual who was faced with an extremely difficult and lonely holiday season. To give just a few details as building blocks to the story, a mother of four children had struggled for years to make her marriage work. There were times in which she and her husband enjoyed each other and the life they had together raising their children. The family was very active and both parents were extremely involved in their children's education, activities, and overall well-being. Individually, both people were dedicated to achieving a common goal, to live a life full of love, joy, and wellness. Sadly, these two souls could no longer journey together in tandem. Their methods and beliefs about how to achieve these goals began to differ too vastly. Soon came the hurt and the resentment. The husband believed that he had endured too much of his wife's seemingly erratic emotions and the wife believed that she felt imprisoned and tortured by her husband's mixed messages, control, and destruction of her spirit.

They tried to make it work but it was too far gone. There was nothing more that they, or anyone, could do and a tough decision had to be made. The wife became the one to make that tough decision, and for that, she paid more of the price. Since there was no space for collaboration left in the husband, he dictated the way things were going to unfold with him, the house, their finances, and their children. The children always felt caught in the middle, unsure of their place in the family, their alliances, managing their own inner conflicts, and sometimes capitalizing on the tension in the home for survival.

During this process the kids felt confused, scared, angry, and unsure.

Who wouldn't? Their parents could not manage each other, so how could the kids manage anything in a healthy way themselves? This fracture was a long time in the making, well before any decision to separate was made. As the story unfolded, the woman found a place to leave nearby, she tried to recreate a home environment as best as she could, but with no job (having been a full-time stay-at-home mother for years), limited savings, and the continued escalating conflict between her and her husband, she found herself feeling powerless, alone, and in a very dark place. The hope of the future kept her going, and the little contact she was granted with the kids gave her moments of strength and clarity. But alas, old patterns of communication, anger, control, and disruption appeared to plague both mother and father. Despite her best efforts to redirect, their differing styles of communicating and operating were too vast to allow this to be a smooth transition.

As Thanksgiving approached that year, she was disappointed again by the realization that she would not be allowed to share the holiday with her children. They had been scheduled in a way that prevented contact with her. Faced with the acceptance that things were not going to go peacefully and smoothly, she decided not to pursue a fight or a power struggle over seeing the kids; she did not wish to put them through that and force the issue. In addition, she felt a tremble in the pit of her stomach with the thought of spending that holiday with parts of her family of origin (her mother and her siblings' families). She faced a dilemma, one that left her feeling powerless, distraught, and hopeless. In our discussion about this, I asked her to focus on a feeling of joy, peace, and excitement for this holiday. To free her mind from the parameters of what is logical, traditional, and expected of her. I asked that she answer this next question impulsively and that she allowed her vision to be articulated without much thought. I asked what would make this holiday special for her given these circumstances. She thought for just a brief moment and said that she always wanted to go to New York City to watch the Macy's Thanksgiving Day Parade but had never been given the opportunity to do that. With a marriage, children, and other family expectations, it was a dream that never came to fruition.

My next response was that she may wish that she never shared this vision with me because I thought it was a brilliant idea, one that was extreme but attainable, and that I would like to encourage her to do that. I admitted that it would be hard for me to let that idea go. I had spent a lot of time with her in prior work, encouraging her to operate outside of her comfort zone, to push herself a bit, and to have some healthy fun. I was so proud of her because as our conversation developed, she seemed more and more open to this idea. She was smiling, she came alive, and for the first time in months, I had seen a giddy joy in her despite the sadness and isolation of her current circumstances. We talked about how she could just simply "do it." She could choose to drive there or to take a train, with no major plans other than to simply be a part of the excitement and celebration. The more she thought of it the more she smiled. It was as if she was in high school planning a senior skip day with her friends. As the next few weeks unfolded, I tried to resist my temptation to ask about updates from her regarding whether or not she was ready for such a bold leap. I mostly encouraged her to stay in this feeling state in comparison to how the holiday was originally shaping up to be.

I also made her a deal that if she could follow through on something of this magnitude, then I would never bring up nudging her outside of her comfort zone again. This act would be so colossal, that it would stop me in my tracks from ever speaking about such things again. To my extreme delight, I woke up on that Thanksgiving morning, just a few weeks after our discussion, and received an email from her. It was a picture of what the parade looked like from the side of the street. At first, I thought it was a brilliantly funny and cute e-mail, that she had remembered our discussion and decided to offer me a little smile as a reminder that she was open to new things in her life. I thought that it was just a random picture from the internet that she shared with me. But then it occurred to me that it was actually a picture from her own cell phone. She had done it, she got on the metro at midnight, arrived in the city in the early morning, spent her time walking around, drinking some hot chocolate, and engaging in some joyful casual discussions with new people. She waited until the city woke up, found a good spot to watch the parade, and even ran into a family from the small town in which she lived. She took a picture, enjoyed herself, and made the voyage back home.

This did not offer me just a quick smile, it made my entire holiday and it gives me chills to this day as I write this passage. Her courage and strength remains inspiring to me and her ability to follow and execute these principles in energy theory was truly remarkable. She was beyond successful because she completely turned her holiday around, and in many ways, I believe she changed her life just in that decision to act on this joyful vision. She was in a place of darkness and solitude and transformed that energy into something magical and unforgettable. Once she freed herself from the upset feeling that she was not in control of spending time with her children that day, and once she freed herself from operating within the boundaries of social expectations and traditions, she was able to move into a creative and intuitive territory that allowed her to experience that holiday in a way that was truly beyond her wildest dreams. While this act of courage and selfcare did not "solve" her problems, it was a strong beginning step that was the equivalent of dropping a pebble in a pond and watching the ripple effect. She needed something monumental to serve as a symbolic shift towards empowerment, independence, and hope.

In another example of honing in the skills of this type of energy work, I would like to share a story of a trip to the mall that I took with my then seven year old son Jake and his granddad. One day in a rare moment of having some guy time, we decided to go to a local mall to walk around, run some errands, and to play arcade claw machines. This was a special treat for Jake because he had developed quite an obsession with claw machines for a couple of years prior and started saving his money to one day buy his own claw machine. He has spent a lot of time keeping this vision in the forefront of his mind; watching claw machine videos on YouTube, doing his own reviews of claw machines, and making claw machine models at home out of cardboard and Legos.

On a side note, the energy flow for us as parents has been to follow this passion with him, to nurture and guide it, and to help him to start cultivating an important lesson in life and in future career directions. We encourage him and support him in his efforts to save his money to one day buy his own arcade claw machine. It is our plan and intention to help him out financially at some point once he reaches most of his goal. I will then help him to learn how to master his skills with the game itself and with repairing and maintaining the machine. It is our plan to put the arcade claw machine on location somewhere so that he will have a taste at running his own business, much like a child opening a lemonade stand. He has already accumulated a couple of bags full of prizes he has won from other claw machines. He plans on using these to fill his machine to get it up and running. We love the fact that he is already showing such a passion for something that he enjoys and that he is looking forward to finding that rare balance between doing what you love, loving what you do, and generating income at the same time. Please keep a look out in the future for Jake's Claw Machines in an area near you :)

Back to the story at hand. On this special trip to the mall, Jake was very well behaved and patient during a couple of the errands we had to run. He did not repeatedly ask to play the claw machines or ask for me to purchase things for him while in other stores. He had done a great job earning several turns at his favorite claw machine spot. He was even successful at one of his attempts to win a stuffed animal and had decided that he would gift it to his little sister who would enjoy the character. The events that unfolded after could easily be described as a wonderful example of tapping into the energy around him and allowing it to flow in a positive direction. Jake was certainly on a roll that day.

As we walked by the small pretzel shop, we were discussing how sweet it was of him to offer this prize to his sister, that it would mean a lot to her and that he would feel good about doing it. We then heard a loud sound as a college aged woman dropped a handful of change in the near distance from us at the pretzel shop. She was with another friend who bent down to help her pick up the change. I heard her say "that's okay, just leave it, I don't really care about it," then they walked away. Jake had certainly heard the change fall and witnessed the woman walking away. I had my arm around his shoulder at the time (because I want to cherish that contact while he lets me before he becomes a teenager) and I felt him pull back for a moment. He stopped and told me that the woman dropped the change and that he wanted to go pick it up and to give it back to her. At first, I was certain that he wanted to pick up the change to put in his pocket, and I was very surprised to hear that he just wanted to be helpful to the woman. I paused for a moment to think about this because I did not want to block his good Samaritan tendencies, yet I heard her clearly that she was not interested in bending down, nor having her friend bend down, to pick up the change. I decided to let his energy flow and felt strongly that it would be good in some way.

We wandered over to the change and I realized that it was a lot more than I initially thought. It was two large handfuls of change for him to carry, maybe adding up to $2 or $3. I noticed what store the woman walked into and offered to walk with Jake as he sought them out and approached them. I kept about a 10 foot distance from him to allow for his independence during this exercise and watched as he found them. He bravely walked up to the beautiful older women and said "excuse me, you dropped your change and I wanted you to have it back." The young woman was stunned for a moment, took the change back, and simply replied with "thanks bud, you didn't have to do that." She went back to her shopping and Jake walked away with a small grin, obviously pleased with himself.

We left the store, again with my arm around his shoulder. I praised him for his good deeds and the importance of being kind to others. I also try to instill a sense a chivalry and respect for women. He was beaming with delight in himself and his behavior. I asked him why he chose to do this and he explained that he thought it was important because the woman dropped her money and he wanted to help her pick it up because it would have taken her a long time to do by herself. I asked if he noticed anything else about her and that interaction. He said that he noticed that she did not seem to want the money she dropped but that maybe it was because it would have been a lot of work to pick it up. While he is typically quick to wonder what he may get out of behaving well, he did not think, expect, or ask for anything in return for his actions. He truly felt the pride in being a

Good Samaritan, or in Jewish culture, doing a mitzvah.

We continued walking in the mall and I thought a bit about what that experience was like for that young woman. She was polite and smiled at Jake with appropriate appreciation and simply said "Oh, thanks bud, you didn't have to do that" as she took the change and walked away. However, something seemed missing and distant within her. She appeared to be simply going through the motions of her day, unfazed by much. It then occurred to me that perhaps that there was meaning in this for her. I quickly had a flash of the many many women I have seen in my practice between the ages of 18-33 years old that seem to have been plagued by low self value, worth, and self image. Women who have been sent messages their entire lives that made them feel blamed, criticized, and not special. Women who have settled for mediocre relationships, jobs, and living situations because that is all they knew, expected, and felt they deserved. So to me, this missing part of the woman at the mall was very familiar to me, I could almost sense it.

I had this energetic and spiritual thought, some may say just a fabrication in my mind, that perhaps the interaction she had with Jake was to introduce her to a sample of how she should be treated. In order for this message to resonate within her, I suspect that this experience needed to come from a non-threatening source, like an innocent, seven year old boy.

I believe that she may have needed a small and subtle introduction of an energetic and cosmic shift in her life. The shift towards the direction of a belief that she is important, that her needs matter and should be attended to, that she should be respected, and that it is valuable to pay attention to little things in life. Though she may not have needed the dollar or so of change, it represented a negligence on her part and an outward example of an inward experience that basic things are not worth it for her. On a fundamental level, if a person drops something, he/she should pick it up. Or, if she works hard to earn her money, she should value and respect how she cares for it, treats it, and uses it. Or, if a person goes out of his/her way to be kind to her, she could spend a little more time acknowledging that and appreciating it.

Not but a few moments later, another young lady was walking with a family member and she had a jacket tied around her waste. As they approached a center focal point/intersection in the mall, they stopped to decide their direction. We were trailing about 100 feet behind and I noticed that her jacket dropped to the ground. Jake had not noticed this yet and I wondered if there would be other people much closer to them to perhaps point out what happened. By the time we arrived at the jacket, Jake noticed it and said "oh, somebody is missing their jacket." I mentioned that I saw who misplaced it and that she was up ahead of us. He scooped it up and jogged ahead to reunite the woman with her jacket. I stayed close enough but gave him his space yet again. Though I could not hear what she said, there was a notable difference in this interaction versus his first one. She was extremely appreciative with a bright smile and demeanor, and her family member appeared to be just as thrilled about the jacket being found and returned. Jake walked back to me with his usual half smile, trying hard to not show how pleased he was but also not able to contain his joy. He got another hug from me and his granddad and we continued on our journey.

I asked him if he noticed anything different about the women in each of the scenarios and he replied that the second person seemed to be much happier about his good deed. He further replied that he thought that the first woman was nice but that maybe she did not really care about having the money back. I agreed with his assessment and asked if that changed anything about his decision and how he handled the situation. He mentioned that he still felt the same way and added that he did not think he should have kept the money because he saw who dropped it. Perhaps it would have been different if there was no one around to claim their loss? Overall, it appeared that energy principles indicated that he was a vessel for good deeds that day and felt the pride associated with helping out others. He accurately assessed what was needed and appropriate in each category, and hopefully had a profound impact on each woman he interacted with. The first one, in a subtle way, and the second in a more overt way. On a side note, I think that energy flowed very well for him that day, starting with the decision to gift his claw machine winning to his younger sister, and followed as he was able to continue this momentum throughout the rest of that trip to the mall.

*Chapter 18*

# Examples of Energy Flow Beyond What You Could Expect/Imagine

There are times in which energy flows in ways that offer continued positive and unexpected effects, further validating that energy was flowing correctly. If we look at the simple act of buying a car, we can see that many people have a routine of what they pay attention to, what guiding principles aid in making a purchase decision, and what offers them comfort and reassurance in a rather large purchase and long term commitment. Buying a car can be stressful and anxiety provoking as people navigate through the process. Often times, people will look at the monthly expense of a vehicle, the function it will perform for them or their family, the make, model, year, mileage, warranties associated with their purchase, and the list goes on. These are all valuable and important things to consider with such a big purchase.

However, I posit that there are other important things that can and should factor into a decision like this, things that may seem anxiety provoking to some. Between the time that the internet was first gaining more mainstream popularity in the late 1990s to currently, I have purchased three used vehicles, sight unseen, from out of state sellers on the internet. No warranties or guarantees, just following energy theory on principles of the meticulous nature of the way in which pictures were taken, the phrasing of the ads, the interaction between myself and the seller, the reason for the sale-what vehicle they were getting to replace this car for sale, and the type of maintenance that was performed.

I have also learned to ask certain questions about the circumstances in which they purchased the car to begin with, and other general philosophies and beliefs they have. To me, it has been just as important to learn as much about the person selling the vehicle (whether that is the owner or dealership) as it has been to learn about the vehicle itself. During my most recent purchase a couple of years ago, it took me over 4 months to find my car. I already had it narrowed down to the year, make and model, and I had seen literally hundreds upon hundreds of ads online, and about a half dozen cars in person to test drive. Though all of those cars fit the criteria, and many often fit the budget, something was amiss in each deal. After finally finding the "right" vehicle and deal for me, I made the purchase sight unseen and began the shipping process. Energy flowed so correctly, that even three years later, I continued to learn about features and capabilities of this vehicle that I did not realize contributed to how great of a purchase I made and how much I enjoy the vehicle every time I drive it.

Before the days of being a family man, I had enjoyed a passion for sports cars and I spent a lot of time working on my vehicles, upgrading them, modifying them, and designing things on them to customize them to my liking. In one example, I had a 1991 Toyota Mr2 turbo, my dream car, and I was actively involved in the Mr2 message board/forum online to share the passion with others, to get help for various mechanical fixes, and to share trials and tribulations of ownership. After performing the finishing touches in modifying the car, I was in "need" of a new exhaust system. I say in "need" with a little smirk because I recognize that it was not an actual "need." After much research and deliberation, I came to the conclusion that I needed to design my own custom exhaust to meet my specifications for function, performance, design, and sound. This is a theme that repeats itself to this day as I have a hard time finding things just the way I want them. I seem to need to modify just about everything that I buy for myself or my vehicles. I do not have the ego or arrogance to believe that I can do it better than the large companies who invest millions of dollars into research and design, it is more so that I have an artistic eye to see what can be tweaked or altered for a more unique way of getting enjoyment out of products.

Regarding the exhaust, I found another member on the Mr2 forum to help me actually build/weld the exhaust. We worked in tandem for a couple of months, communicating back and forth via email regarding the details and specifications. I chose specific dual mufflers, the size of the piping, the angles and layout of system, the exhaust tips to use, etc. He was so masterful with his craftsmanship that together, we turned out a product that remains to this day, the highest proven horsepower gain exhaust in production for that car. Personally, this was an example of a triumphant moment and an added unexpected benefit of energy flow. I did not set out to make the best exhaust in terms of highest performance, I did not intend for the design to be liked by so many others, and I did not intend or ask for any part of profits that the other member gained in continuing to produce this exhaust for others. For me, it was exactly what "I" wanted and I enjoyed every moment of looking at it, hearing it, and feeling its performance. However, because I took my time with it, because I found the right person with the skill and attention to detail that I had, energy flow allowed this creation to offer him greater income and business, as well as countless other people the joy of this exhaust. It is a fun little secret for me to know that I helped design the top performing exhaust for a vehicle that I love with great passion.

## Chapter 19

# Using Energy Theory in Mechanical Repairs, Fixing by Sense

As you can tell by now, I am a car guy (and motorcycle guy too) and over the years, I have been able to acquire a fair amount of self taught mechanical knowledge. I have turned a wrench or two in my time resulting in good amount of bloody knuckles but also a lot of pride in knowing that I did a good job on a repair and saved money in the process. On a side note, I highly recommend that all drivers know how to change a tire and plug a flat tire on the side of the road. One important reason is that being more capable of handling issues and problems on your own will help you to minimize the effects a crisis situation can have. In addition, not only can you save money and time, but you can also operate "in tune" and "in oneness" with your vehicle; similar to the life saving art of the motorcycle repair that my client helped to bring to my attention.

With that said, I believe in the power of energy theory so much that I am working towards a goal of becoming somewhat of a "car whisperer." I admit that I am not a certified mechanic but I have learned to pay attention to the sounds and "feel" of a car so much that I have challenged several mechanics with decades of experience about certain diagnostic issues I've encountered. On most occasions I have found myself to be accurate despite their logic and experience.

I do not wish to criticize others in any way or speak about this with any arrogance. I merely wish to describe another practical use for energy theory, even as it relates to car repairs. Consider for a moment if you have ever experienced a time in which your car was running well, then the check engine light comes on, then the next you thing you know it costs you somewhere between $300-900. Something instinctively told you that this does not make sense, it is not like the car left you on the side of the road, yet, this was considered to be a simple repair. You do not have to know a lot about cars to use your logic and intuition to guide you in this process. As with all things, I am recommending that you pay attention to the signs and signals around you. Sometimes a part does cost several hundred dollars or even just the labor to install it. Yet, there are other times in which that check engine light can be remedied with a $35 oxygen sensor that can take 15 minutes to install with the right tool.

Going back to the recent car purchase example, I have realized that despite my progression from sports car to a family SUV large enough to carry three car seats, music still remains important to me and I could not resist my urge to upgrade my stereo sound system by adding an amplifier and sub-woofer for better bass response. To put it simply, it makes me feel better when my music goes "boom" and it shakes my seats. I am still a kid inside when it comes to that.

During my pursuits to research and explore what I would get, my budget, and how I would go about completing this project, I labored with the tough decision to do the installation myself versus having it professionally installed. I have installed many car stereos before, so I knew the involvement, the financial savings, the joy/satisfaction, and the stress that comes with it. It was a tug of war between my schedule, my finances, and deciding how to best install and wire the amplifier and sub-woofer to my system. I finally made the tough decision to try and let go of the complication, the stress, and the control of the situation and I sought out a local company to install the equipment if I brought it to them.

This was a tough decision because there were several options as to how to wire this into the stereo system and I spent a lot of time doing the research to try to figure out which way was best. I realized that I was short circuited and that I needed to "let go," to simply drop off my car and have faith that it would be done correctly and it would all work out. So, that is what I did. However, when I picked my car back up and drove it home, I was not very impressed with the performance. It took me a day or so to get used to the change in the system and to determine if I thought this came out the way that I wanted it to. I began to obsess again and fixated on how this was wired, if there was a better way, if I needed to change the set up I planned on, etc. I tried very hard to resist the temptation to invest more time into this project, trying to be mindful of energy theory principles. Within another week or so, I decided that the space in my SUV must have been bigger than I realized and that I needed two sub-woofers to effectively achieve what I wanted to. So, I put effort into trying to "tweak" the system. I added another sub-woofer and did not have to change wiring, the amplifier, or anything else.

This set up "seemed" to work well for me for about a week or two. Then it started to make loud speaker noises after start up of my vehicle (with or without the stereo on). At first, I was so stressed about the entire ordeal that I decided to try to ignore this problem, hoping that it would go away. But alas, it became worse until I had no choice but to pay attention to it. I was convinced this was some type of punishment for wanting to upgrade my stereo to begin with. After spending more time researching the problem, I could not get online car stereo forums to agree on this issue, nor the person who installed the system, nor the manufacturer of the sub-woofer and amplifier, nor the company that sold me the equipment, nor another known car stereo vendor. I was left with no one but myself and my father to do our head scratching diagnosis of the system.

Within a mere 45 minutes or so of doing some of our own tests and trials of wiring and rewiring, we came across something that we were not expecting. Namely, that we fixed this system in a way that was better than imagined or hoped for. After investing our own diagnostic time into this and using the blend of our intellect with our intuition, the system was so much louder and efficient that I was able to turn down the power on the amplifier, remove the extra sub-woofer (going back to the plan of only one) and this system was still louder, more crisp, and accurate than it ever was from the beginning of this project. It was as if all the stars lined up to make this system better than anything that I thought was possible. To this day, I am reminded of how wonderful this success turned out to be with every note that comes out of that speaker. It is hard to describe but there is something blissful about enjoying something every single time that it is used, never taking its purpose for granted, not even for one moment. It is even more gratifying knowing that I was able to accomplish something that multiple experts in the car stereo industry could not.

I spent about two months invested into this very stressful project, trying to mindfully follow all of the signs and signals in front of me. It was complex and required more than just intellect, skill, deductive reasoning, and intuition. It was guided by something else. And though it may seem trivial, the end result made moments of agony, frustration, hopelessness, and despair all worth it. I had a system that performed beyond my dreams and that allowed me to experience music that I enjoy and to "feel" the sound. This has culminated in my belief system and goal that if harnessed correctly, energy theory can be used so effectively that one could almost diagnose or fix problems with inanimate objects just by being in its presence or having the senses open enough to "understand" something just by touching it. While that appears to be an impossible task, this is something that I believe is attainable and worthy of pursuit.

## Chapter 20

# Using Energy Theory in Separation and Divorce

As we know, the divorce rate in our country sadly hovers just over 50% and it is a consistent and upsetting reason why people seek my services in private practice. It is common for people to struggle with questions like:

1. If they love their partner anymore.

2. If there was ever a true love to begin with, how did they drift apart.

3. If it can be regained/recaptured.

4. How to they go about the details of separating.

5. If there are kids involved, how they can separate and remain partners in parenting for the rest of their children's lives.

Utilizing energy theory, I hope to offer a small example of a template for people to use that would allow them to acknowledge a connection that once was, a sadness that things have changed over time, a recognition that both people had a responsibility in creating hurts and divisive wedges, and a desire to release each other. It is very possible that, using this philosophy, two people can decide to separate/divorce so that they can save their relationship; a relationship built on a foundation of mutual care and respect for the other.

To clarify, "saving a relationship" does not necessarily suggest staying together in a romantic relationship. I believe that a couple can save a relationship even if they have no desire to remain in contact or be tied to each other. In addition, I believe that a couple can save a relationship if they have children and will be co-parenting in the present and future. In a scenario of not wanting to see or to speak to each other again, the relationship that is being "saved" would be the memory of the former relationship. There was some positive at one point and the use of this energy theory could help preserve those memories.

Imagine the impact if people could travel back in time to speak to their former selves to implement principles of energy theory. Perhaps they could show their former selves that hate and disdain does not have to overshadow what brought them together. They could convey a sense of love and enough care for each other to end the romantic relationship before it turned their hearts cold and dark. I completely understand that this concept may sound lofty and rose colored. I do not wish to dismiss the hurts and wounds people have endured in their relationships. However, I merely hope to illustrate just one example of a way to handle a separation/divorce from a symbolic and spiritual perspective.

Regarding the scenario in which there are children, here is an example to map out an approach for couples to consider. This could serve as a guide for a basic fundamental belief system and a way to present this:

> "I have put a lot of thought into us lately and there are some very important things that I wish to share with you. I hope that you can give me a chance to say these things and to hear them as coming from a loving place in my heart.
>
> For almost _____ years I have loved you. We have created a life together and have had _____ wonderful children (if applicable). They have given me more purpose in my life and for that, I am forever grateful. You have dedicated yourself to working hard to contribute to our household, to support me/us, and to create a lifestyle in which our children could have better opportunities than we had at their age. I feel strongly that I have dedicated myself to that same goal as well.
>
> Our love story has not ended with a "happily ever after." There has been pain, sadness, anger, and hurt. Sadly, this has been by each of our hands. I am not sure when, but some time ago, we lost our way. I think that we got stuck in our roles in the family and in our individual identity. The foundation of what we built our relationship on slipped through the cracks; life got in the way. I pushed these feelings down, I kept them away, and I spent a lot of time trying to convince myself that I "should" be happy, I have many things that most people would want. But there was something missing, an emotional connection and partnership that made me feel better as a person, one that uplifted my spirit and made me feel like I was important. I do not want to blame you for that or say that it is all your fault. I just want to share what had been eroding away inside of me for quite some time.

I allowed this feeling inside to grow without paying much attention to it. Then, I felt sad, I felt alone, I was being criticized for my attempts to communicate and reach out to you. So, I withdrew more inward, I isolated from you and thought I could live in that state of deprivation. I am sure you felt the same way too, maybe I seemed cold or distant? It is hard to admit this but there were subtle things that I became aware of that was missing in our relationship. I would read books, watch movies, or television, and even see how some couples interacted in public, and these quiet moments smacked me in the face with the harsh reality that I did not have a partner to share those intimate and trivial things with. There were times in which I just could not give to you, I could not be attentive, and I could not reach out to you. There are things that I am not proud of, and there are also things that you have said and done that have left permanent scars in my heart.

The purpose of writing this letter and speaking to you in this way is to start a healing path for us and for our family. Also, to release the things from the past and to open a possibility to forge a new relationship, one that allows us to love and give to each other in a different way, one that allows us to accept each other as individuals, and one that allows us to be partners in parenting. I cannot make any proclamations or promises about what will or will not happen in the future, I just know that it is clear to me that we need to be a part so that we can continue to care for each other and to be there for our children. We are hurting each other and I cannot see any other way of healing. It is my hope that you understand that what may appear to be the beginning of the end, is really a chance to salvage what is left in our hearts. It may not be under the same roof, it may not be in the context of a marriage, but it will certainly be in honor of what brought us together almost _____ years ago and what will forever keep us tied together. The cycle of hurt, pain, mistrust, criticism, and negativity needs to stop. It is not fair to any of us living in the house to breathe in the toxic air of what has occurred in our past and what is both spoken and unspoken in the walls of our home.

Let us please work together to figure out the options and logistics that may best work for all of us, my heart is at peace with you, not war…………I hope the same is true for you.

With Love,


Again, this is merely an example or template to guide people in their efforts to heal, to start over, to separate, or to even reconnect. Even if these things do not apply directly to you, the spirit within this sample can still serve as a realistic way to communicate strong feelings without anger or attack. I would never guarantee or predict how a person would react to hearing such a sentiment if they were being told this by their spouse or partner. I would, however, suggest that there is a part of them that could hear the love and consideration for their feelings in this. They may not directly react to that in a positive way, but there is something inside of them whispering in their ear that the writer is heartfelt and truthful. Taking the time to communicate in this clear and considerate way allows there to be the space and opportunity for connecting discussion. It would be an energetic error to assign success or failure during an experience like this by how a person reacts or if they agree or can be nice and collaborate. The goal and task would be for the reader to tap into that peaceful balance within and to set the stage for how he/she will proceed. Things still may end up adversarial, utilizing attorneys, mediators, etc, to guide the process.

*Chapter 21*

# Importance of Vulnerability

In order to achieve a fulfilling level of intimacy with people we care about in all categories of relationships (romantic, emotional, family, etc), the key ingredient appears to be based on a foundation of vulnerability. If we stop and think about it for a moment, consider any relationship you have had in your life that has been meaningful and fulfilling; it is likely to hinge upon some level of vulnerability and openness. In addition, if you consider for a moment any relationship that has been hurtful or not fulfilling, there is likely to have been some form of a block or hesitancy to be vulnerable. I define vulnerability in the context of energy theory as a willingness to take some calculated risks in sharing, opening up, communicating, and in self-awareness. There is typically a negative connotation associated with being "vulnerable" but I suggest that there is such a thing as healthy vulnerability: not allowing fear, insecurity, and doubt to paralyze healthy emotional growth, communication, and connection to others.

One of the most important ingredients in a psychotherapy relationship between the therapist and client is that of willingness and tolerance for vulnerability within the room. Often times, the implication is that it goes one way, that it is a one sided relationship in which the therapist exists as the professional who is there for the sole purpose of the client and to offer his/her psychological and emotional support and guidance. However, there are times in which self-disclosure from the therapist can be enhancing to the professional relationship as it humanizes the therapist, fosters trust and sometimes even credibility that he/she can relate to the joy or struggles of the other person in the room. This next section will illustrate an example of using energy theory to address three things: struggling with personal obstacles, being vulnerable to one's partner/spouse, and self-disclosure by a therapist in the context of the psychotherapeutic relationship.

As I write this section, I continue to practice taking a safe and calculated risk in being open and vulnerable to others. I will reveal things about myself that were once kept in very dark corners deep within. These are things that were once virtually impossible for me to say out loud, hearing myself say the words made it too real and upsetting. It remains quite difficult at times, but I am finding more control over my emotional reactions with each act of vulnerability; using energy theory to reduce the power that triggers can have over me.

Working backwards in the time line for this example, I recently had several skin growths removed from my face leaving scabs for several weeks and red marks for several months. The growths came from a skin condition called sebaceous hyperplasia and were essentially overactive oil gland growths. At first, they appeared to be acne blemishes, then some type of cyst or mole. The dermatologist said that they were not cancerous or problematic to my health, only a genetic skin condition that is a cosmetic nuisance to people. She cauterized them with a special tool, which was extremely painful but only lasted a moment for each one, and told me that they should heal in a couple of weeks. So far this story may sound fairly benign or trivial. Essentially, the classic tale of getting older and not being happy with the changes your body is going through. For me, however, it was much more involved and pervasive than that.

The several months leading up to having these growths removed were among the most difficult that I can remember since my youth. The internal struggle was so intense that I could barely take it, fighting inside to find a way to block these feelings of insecurity, anxiety, anger, and fear while trying to be genuinely present for others (clients and family). A very difficult task under normal circumstances, let alone when you feel so embarrassed that you want to hide under the covers in a very dark room. My history with facial skin conditions started when I was 13. I thought that perhaps it was going to be some transitional hormonal acne but it was much more severe and pervasive than that. I spent the next six years going to dermatologist appointments trying the next idea of medication to help treat this condition.

Sadly, these attempts and trials proved unhelpful and I never experienced the relief that I so longed for. During this time, I experienced a deep depression that I could not share with anyone. Though my pain was evident on the outside, and in my mood/outlook, I could not speak the words out loud as to what was bothering me. I tried many times but it was as if the words could not literally escape my lips. I felt a small sense of relief at night time when it became easier to hide in the shadows. I also felt a very small amount of relief while wearing sunglasses. I knew that I did not suddenly become invisible when I wore them, but I felt a little safer if people could not see into my eyes. I felt as if they could read my thoughts if they could look into my eyes, sense my pain, and somehow know what was most upsetting to me. In addition, I also could not bare to take the risk of catching someone staring at me or noticing my poor skin. Looking people in the eye was a very vulnerable thing that I could not bare at the time.

I spent most of my time during the day longing to look different, envious of people who were not afflicted with this, bargaining with God about what I would give up if I could be healed, and trying to reassure myself that this would not last forever. I even used to keep track on my calendar when I had very "bad skin days" and would see the pattern in a given month of having typically no more than 1-4 sporadic days in a month in which I could "tolerate" my appearance. Most other days were considered to be bad and unbearable. It got so bad that I avoided using certain words that would upset me, even if they were used in a different context; words like clear, face, skin, swollen, red, acne, blemish, scar, mark-essentially anything that reminded me of my upsetting appearance. Another thing that plagued me was looking into mirrors, it became so upsetting to see my reflection that I noticed the parallel between myself and mythical vampires who avoided the sun, people, and mirrors.

There were times in which my skin flare ups were so bad that people often wondered if I had gotten into a fight or if I had an allergic reaction to foods or chemicals or if I had gotten stung by bees. I would often had large swollen marks on my face that were painful and red. After many years, the flare ups lessened some and gave me slightly longer periods of tolerance. However, nothing cured me or got rid of these conditions and I remained upset about my appearance more often than not. This continued for the next 20 years, culminating in the more recent experience described above; a couple of skin growths and my decision to have them attended to by a dermatologist. Though I worked through some of the issues from my past with this, I had continued patterns of behavior that contributed to my stress and frustration. I struggled with dealing with memories of an awkward childhood and continued feelings of sadness and frustration during flare ups, avoidance of people and situations, a dependency on utilizing some of my wife's blemish concealer to mask redness, and a hyper awareness of lighting and angles-anything that would aide me in the pseudo realm of hiding/masking. By the time I made it to the dermatologists office, I was defeated, hopeless, and anxious once again. My foundation was rocked and everything from the past came flooding back to me. I had the skin growths removed painfully without local anesthetic, which I welcomed as a way to manage the aggression inside about this.

During the first day of healing, the marks got worse and I started to panic about how I would look in another day or so when the weekend was over and I went back to work. I could not use a concealer because I was healing and I was not ready to face the world again. The next 48 hours became very important because I tried very hard to think about what energy theory would dictate in this process and how I would handle this if I was counseling someone in my situation. Practicing what I preach, I made an extremely tough decision to continue to see people in appointments as scheduled and to be open and direct about my appearance and experience. I realized that it was not anyone else's "need" to have things explained or revealed, yet I determined that I could reduce the power the situation had over me by saying it out loud, by being vulnerable, and releasing the behavior of hiding and angst. This was not an easy task for me and it remains an intense source of discomfort even as I write this now.

It started by talking to my wife, my best friend, and revealing to her how much of an impact all of this has had on me. She had known me for 18 years at the time and had some sense of my internal struggles. Despite how close we have been, I never revealed "everything" to her, especially the part about feeling so unlovable that I wondered how she could be with me despite my appearance. The freedom that I felt by this disclosure was immeasurable and unpredictable to me. I *knew* that it would be helpful and necessary, but I had no idea how important it was to both of us; bringing us closer together and allowing my heart to feel loved and nurtured by her caring and nurturing energy. After that, I wrote this suggestion for people to consider on my Inner Journey Counseling Center Facebook page:

> Feeling stuck in frustration, anger, hurt? Here is quite an extreme challenge to help free yourself from circumstances beyond your control. It is a simple concept, not easy to do, and it is likely you will think that it won't "work."
>
> I suggest an extreme act of vulnerability, share with whomever you consider to be your very best friend (hopefully, someone you live with) this dark place that you are in. Share the frustration, the anger, the hurt, how unfair it is, and the desire to release it. Speak this truth in a raw and honest way, in a way that you never have shared before. If you are not tearful during this exercise, you may not be doing it right. Dig down deep and share something that you cannot bare to say

out loud, something that is tough for you to even think about.

Try this with that special person you keep very close to your heart. He/she will not have the answers and will only be able to love, hug, comfort, and reassure. Ironically, that is not the thing that is most helpful in this exercise. The most helpful thing that will allow you to feel a release, and to free yourself from that invisible prison, is your act of vulnerability.

Holding things in for too long contributes to your feelings of sadness, depression, isolation, and hopelessness. This will help you with the beginning steps toward healing. You will then soon be able to focus and to work on strategies and solutions using your intellect, your heart, your intuition, and your spirit.

Good luck with sharing!

The next difficult task for me came with preparing for each appointment that I had during the upcoming week. I started off with something to the effect of:

"Please excuse my appearance, I had some skin growths removed by the doctor and I am in the healing process. The best way for me to deal with insecurity and upset is to be direct and upfront about it. I just needed to say this out loud."

During those moments people were supportive, understanding, and made attempts to be comforting by telling me that they had not noticed until I pointed it out. Some asked more questions and some did not. The point of this was not to get support or to hear responses of reassurance, it was merely to say something out loud so that I could reduce its power over me and to release it enough so that I could be present for others in that moment. Remarkably, this worked fairly well for me despite how difficult it was. I felt more freedom that I had in years, and though I continued to struggle with satisfaction about my appearance, I was grateful for the shift in energy that I was able to achieve. I found that the key to this sense of freedom was the willingness to be vulnerable, to share, and to be direct and honest. I merely adopted the position that I did not wish to hide or to live in this invisible prison any longer.

I have so much more work to do in this category, but as with most things, there is value in the statement "practice, not perfection." It is my belief that sharing this story may aid in the energy shift necessary to help me feel more like myself. Writing these things, speaking them, and confronting them directly has been one of the most difficult things of my life. There have been many more upsetting episodes since I began to share this story about myself. I felt like I have been brought to the brink of destruction, yet, I continued to fight this war, armed with the weapon of this energy theory. I am using it to operate in complete mindfulness, presence in the here and now, simplicity, and peaceful existence. I speak the truth when I say how difficult this task is. There have been many days of darkness and despair. Yet, I also speak the truth when I say how worth it this can be when you allow yourself to confront things deep down within and take the risk to be vulnerable.

# Chapter 22

# Final Thought

I want to sincerely thank you from the deepest part of my heart for allowing my voice to be heard in this way. I hope that this book gives you other tools to consider as you navigate through emotions, reactions, and thoughts connected to things that affect you both internally and externally. After years of observing certain connections both in my profession and in my personal life, I felt compelled to write them down in a cohesive way. I hope that I have done that here. Using energy theory to help guide me, I only wrote the contents of this book when I felt compelled to and moved to do so. I wrote these thoughts with the belief that it did not matter to me how this book got published or what would happen along this journey. Instead, I wrote it with the belief that the book simply had to be brought into existence. That is as far as I went in my thinking. It was my job to write this book and to metaphorically drop the pebble in the pond to see what the ripple waves looked like. This belief system allowed me to write in a way that allowed ideas and concepts to flow without much interference or distraction from my own thoughts (I am prone to over-thinking things).

I truly hope that this book will speak to those of an energetic and spiritual mindset. I would consider it a great honor if it stimulates more thought and discussion for people of this mindset and other mindsets as well. Hopefully, this book can help some people with different mindsets to have an expansive view of how things <u>can</u> work within them and around them on other levels. I would encourage you to re-read this book as a "tune up" when you see fit and perhaps share it with others who can add to discussion about these concepts. I firmly believe in the importance of dialogue that challenges views and helps to promote growth for everyone engaged in discussion.

I would also like to suggest that you look at my Inner Journey Counseling Center Facebook page to view updated general mantra's and thoughts. I have included some from the page here below:

*1) Goal, predict that there will be people that cross your path, intentional or not, who will create static noise to distract you. This is not designed to upset, they are disrupted and "short-circuited." Expect and prepare so that, when it happens, your response is "and there it is" instead of "that makes me mad." In this philosophy, your tools will be sharpened and you will be prepared to adapt to anything around you.*

*2) As the season changes, notice the things that are in transition within you and around you. Try to find your inner grounding with a belief system that allows you to control how you react to things. Remind yourself that you are worthy of peace in your mind and heart and that all you need deep within your core is love and connection from those who enhance your energy, not hinder it.*

*Prepare for unpleasant changes and for an emotional state of not feeling like yourself, feeling swept away in a tornado. This is not really you, it is negative energy flowing, fear of the changes occurring, and the social climate around you. Please do not mistake this for who you are inside; it is false and temporary. Protect your inner peace at all costs! The best way to fight can be by doing nothing, reacting to nothing, and by only allowing things in your life that give you good energy.*

*Operate in compassion today, compassion for others and compassion deep within yourself. Finding stillness within yourself can offer anchoring and confidence in finding your voice.*

*3) Try to focus on helping things to go right versus putting energy into dealing with things when they go wrong. It is not about ignoring the things that could go wrong, but rather, investing in what needs to occur for things to right. Operate with peace in your heart and peace in your intentions.*

*4) The problems in front of us can be viewed as opportunities to make an adjustment or change. They are likely to be upsetting and disruptive but you can find the solutions within by striving for a balance of tapping into your inner spirit/intuition, mixed with following the signs and signals each step of the way. It is tough, but it requires openness to change, patience, more patience, letting go/releasing energy, and the very strategic application of persistence. There is quite a fine art to problem solving but this is a potential equation for starting the process.*

*5) It seems important right now to work on "letting go energy." This is not to say that we should "forgive and forget" (forgetting is extremely dismissive to our experiences) or that letting go of things is somehow condoning or allowing the negative things that occur. It is more so about the idea of sparing yourself from spinning in the mud or ruminating over things that already happened or things that were/are out of our control. The serenity prayer seems to be very appropriate right now. God grant me the serenity to accept the things I cannot change, the courage to change the things I can, and the wisdom to know the difference.*

*6)    There are some very very special people out there that are being hurt by others, being dismissed, misunderstood, and even criticized. Please do not listen to the negativity, please ground yourselves with the comfort that there are people in this world that really do get you and who love and honor your spirit. There is so much occurring right now that derails people from their path. Try to find the confidence within yourself to stay your course, to operate in compassion, and to stay in the light. It is easier to operate in darkness, this is why so many people get trapped by it. The pure and innocent things deep down inside of you may be getting targeted right now. This is false and do not let it crush you! Please know these truths as you read these words. This is meant for every special person who has access to read this. Please feel free to share with anyone you think needs to hear this message.*

*7)    If you are reading this, you have so much value to offer others. Chances are, you are a caregiver, a nurturer, a healer, a self-sacrificer. You are sensitive and attentive to the needs of others. However, you get run down by life, you sometimes get hurt by others, and you can feel that you get little return from the loved ones that you gift your positive energy. Slow down and allow your body and your thoughts to achieve balance. You can do this by finding stillness within. Not everyone can receive your light, be careful who you show it to. We have to filter to get to people who will enhance us, not drain us like an "energy vampire."*

*Pass this along to other people who may not readily see it. Let them know that you love them and that it is your intent to help them in a very small way, via a message of care and nurturing. Take your time tomorrow with your families and friends, enjoy the sounds of nature, the changing smell and scenery, and explore your creativity!*

*8) Adapting to circumstances beyond our control is very tough. Let us be grateful for the health and well-being of our loved ones. Perhaps these circumstances beyond our control serve as opportunities to regroup and to behave in ways that are more consistent with our core and how we intend to operate.*

*9) Please pass along love, warmth, and compassion to all people around you. See people as humans and worthy of your time, your tolerance, and your positive energy. Humanity seems to be a good word to use....Namaste!*

*10) We have the ability to catch how far and how fast we slip into dark places. We can develop the skill to master this more effectively with practice and patience. One way is to write down our thoughts and feelings. Allow the experience to be cathartic and then view your writing as a healing agent. Then, let it go, release it to your higher power and then put energy into the here and now. Try to stay as present as you can. Stay productive and focused as much as you can. If you can soften the impact of a slip into darkness by even just a small percentage, then you have done yourself a great service. Pat yourself on the back for a job well done! Practice not perfection! You are all loved, cared for, and important to so many!*

*11) As the holidays approach, some feel overwhelmed with tasks, schedules, family contact, obligations, and expectations. Let us all try to operate with simplicity as we navigate through the tough decisions about how to manage these stressors. Many people often say that these holidays represent family, unity, peace, and celebration. That is not the case for everyone, for some, this time of year brings sadness, hurt, frustration, and despair. Regardless of the how you feel about this time of year, please consider taking time to reflect on your life in order to work on changing the things that you can, and to value and appreciate the beautiful things in your life that rejuvenate you and keep you going.*

*Please also consider making decisions that honor your spirit, and that nurture you in healthy ways first. Then consider the close circle of the people you keep close to your hearts. Self care is critical this time of year as people often self sacrifice under the belief that it is the "right thing to do." Giving is beautiful, it is divine, and it is essential to the soul. Yet, giving too much, or giving in ways that deplete you is counter productive. It may "feel" selfish to pull back a bit and it may even being upsetting to others, but please, please, pace yourself and consider simplicity.*

*12) Peace in your heart is the key to grounding and cosmic protection. If there are people that are upset with you or upset with your decisions, try to release the pain and hurt that comes with feeling criticized and misunderstood. Forgive them by detaching with love and working on grounding yourself with the awareness that it is not your intention to hurt and that you just want simplicity.*

*13) If you are reading this, you are sensitive, compassionate, and have purity in your heart. You may need to hear these words of support and encouragement. You are a caregiver and you just want the people you love to be happy and healthy. Sometimes people misunderstand that about you, they may misinterpret it, and they may even dismiss, devalue, and abuse. You know what is true in your reality. Please let this message resonate in your mind and heart.*

*Enjoy what you can and remember how special you are and how hard you work everyday to love and cherish others around you. Please pass this along to anyone you believe need to hear this message. However, be selective, this does not apply to everyone.*

*14) If you are feeling run down, drained, and depleted, there is a reason. Things are changing around you, both on the energetic/spiritual level and on the internal level. You are reacting to shifts that are occurring that are beyond your control. It does not have to be scary and it does not have to defeat you. It is a neutral phenomenon and it is up to each of us to be affected either in positive or negative ways. If you are reading this, then you have the ability deep within to experience*

195

*these changes in a more positive way. However, keep in mind that you cannot actively "do" right now, you have to nurture yourself and your body, slow down and practice stillness. In fact, you can make an active choice to "not do." You can opt out of the stressful things birthed from the obligations or expectations put on you by others, by this time of year, and sometimes by yourself. Try to not be reactive to those around you. Some people are aware of these changes and some are not. Let others journey in their own way right now and focus on envisioning a time in the near future in which you will have more energy, more focus, more clarity, and more simplicity.*

*15) Let us all find peace deep within ourselves during our individual pain and during our national tragedies. Let us use our collective desire to co-exist in harmony with those we hold close to our hearts, and certainly those we keep in prayer and thought in our nation. You can find a way to strengthen from within and that will have a profound impact on how you feel, think, and behave during the next few weeks. It will also have an impact on those around you; perhaps in direct or subtle ways, but it will have an impact.*

*16) As we adjust to the aftermath of the holidays, the changing year, the tragedies in society, the political and economic concerns, we need to allow ourselves some breathing room. Please give yourself the freedom and time to feel a little "off". This is not permanent, there is a lot that has recently occurred and a lot that we are still in the midst of. Many people are feeling unbalanced, uncertain, and hopeless. This is not coming from deep within you, it is external and we are allowing ourselves to be affected by it. That is okay for right now, but try to not let it linger too long. Stay in the moment as much as possible.*

*Try to enjoy the simple things that give even a ounce of joy, peace, and respite (as long as they are healthy things). Let us collectively look at rebuilding in the next few weeks and gear up for 2013 to be a strong spiritual shift in our collective consciousness. Please spread kindness, patience, and hope. We can do this!*

*17) Challenge for the day- Write the script for your future, the future that is later today, later this weekend, and later this year or decade. You get to decide how this looks, therefore, you cannot be wrong about the outcome. It may be difficult to envision something clear and positive. That is okay, take your time and use your imagination. Try not to think of logic and practicality. Questions like, how will this come to be? How likely is this outcome? These questions should be disregarded because if you do not believe in the possibility of influencing and guiding yourself to the life you want to have, then you are correct, it will not happen.*

*When we take the risk to be an active observer of ourselves, we find two things that occur. The first is arriving at a genuine truth about ourselves and how we think and behave. The second is that we find ourselves fatigued.*

*Yes, it can be a tiresome road to be mindful of so much, to pay attention to ourselves and the things around us. Yet, we will see the complexity of the world with much more simplicity. It will give us the self protective skill to know when to detach and redirect and when to be open and engaging. You will become more proficient at this and it will become an automatic and natural way for you to process information.*

*This investment is worth while because we are in a constant state of evolution and change. Those who struggle most in life spend a tremendous amount of time and effort trying to keep things the same, trying to not see what is within them and around them. If you are reading this, you more than likely have the strength and courage to challenge yourself and are open to learning more about ways to better yourself.*

*Most people seem to avoid this type of reflecting, take a moment to be proud of yourself for being one of the very few that travels this path. Take just a moment and then get back to your self work . We need more people to continue to think and behave in these ways. Go with peace in your mind and love in your heart, yet vigor in your spirit.*

*There is always room for humbleness and acceptance of our shortcomings. However, there is very little room for doubt about our intentions and the decisions we make when we are operating from deep within the purity of our spirit.*

*18) Speak your truth.....YOUR truth, the one inside of you that you know in your heart of hearts is right for you. Speaking this truth means to have the dialogue from deep within. Keep it as a special secret close to your heart. There are few who will truly understand and support you. Share it with those you can trust, but share very little with those who will criticize and destroy.*

*Your truth is just for you. Walk this path with peace and confidence and be gentle. Make decisions that compliment your unique balance of intellect and emotion. You get to write the script to that story.*

*19) It may be the right time to act on things that are based on your gut instinct and intuition. Strike while the iron is hot and do not hesitate to do what seems right to you in the moment. However, please exercise caution and responsibility. This suggestion is not a license to be impulsive or reckless. Manifesting energy seems to be flowing for those who demonstrate worthiness and modesty. See of you can catch the tail end of this flow, it comes and goes in waves.*

*20) Integrity is the honesty, truthfulness, and accuracy of a person's actions. Your integrity is YOURS, you get to define it, you are responsible for it, and you get to use it in the way that works best for you.*

*Think about the integrity of your thoughts, your actions, and your intentions. Protect it and set the example for those around you.*

*21) Things are unfolding rapidly right now in ways that are overwhelming and somewhat out of control. Slow things down for yourself, create some breathing room and let things marinate a tad before making any major decisions right now. Trust that you will be guided, internally and externally, towards positive things. However, you have to slow down to hear the whisper of the guidance. Trust your intuition, but not necessarily your initial gut reaction to something (unless the gut reaction is concerning your safety and well-being).*

*There are many things for us to pay attention to right now. However, there are very few things that we should be reactive to right now. If you feel like something is off lately, it is because you are right. People are finding themselves extremely distraught and powerless lately.*

*We are either making poor decisions that are destructive to ourselves and those around us, or we are reacting with intense upset emotion and it is holding us down for the count. The goal for now would be to find a third option of neutrality which looks like being aware, attentive, and to detach from reactions with compassion. It is certainly not easy but it is a more peaceful path.*

*22) A brief thought on love....Sometimes it can take a lot of effort to love. The feeling of love is easy, the concept is simple, but the behavior of love can be difficult and draining.*

*When you love another, try to remember why that person is special to you, your*

*first memories together, how the love grew, and what you cherish most about that relationship, romantic partnership, or friendship. What can you do to enhance and nurture that love right now? What can YOU do right now?*

*There are times when you are hurt and frustrated in which you need to speak your inner truth. Times when you owe it to each other to be direct and honest. However, there are other times when things are better left unspoken, not ignored or forgotten, but instead, released due to a mindful conscious decision to not hurt the other and to not linger in negativity.*

*Try hard to know when to choose which option. Perhaps the "serenity prayer" could be helpful in assisting with this decision?*

*God grant me the serenity to accept the things I cannot change, the courage to change the things that I can, and the wisdom to know the difference.*

*Peaceful and loving thoughts are intended for all those that read and share this message.*

*23)  Listen to your body, if you are tired and drained, not able to get enough rest to feel refreshed, SLOW DOWN.  This tends to be a busy time of year for families with children.  Finishing up the school year, sports seasons beginning or winding down, summer preparations for activities, camps, vacations, etc.  Just a small reminder to force time for nothingness.  You cannot wait for it, you can choose to say "no" to certain things and give yourself and your family a day or two here and there to wake up with no plans.  Allow spontaneity to have a chance to guide the family to some special quality time, whether that be on a walk, at home, watching a family movie, etc.*

*Please do not wait for that opportunity to come because it likely will get passed over for some other scheduled or even unscheduled event or commitment.  Your children need to see you take leadership of self care and slowing down with the family.  Yes, they will want to do most of the things you have scheduled, but then again, they will want to eat candy and ice cream every night before bed as well.  Show them the value of time with out electronics and without goal driven activities.  And, show them the value of projects around the house and taking the time to enjoy each other's company.*

*24)   Have you ever thought of something so extreme, so exciting, and so rejuvenating to the soul but felt it was so far out of reach?*

*Have you ever come across an idea that you said in jest, but once you put more thought into it, it sounded like a great idea?*

*What happened next?  Well, you probably decided it was crazy or too difficult or just a dream.  And like most of us, let the thought drift by.  In those moments, we stumble upon a blend of our positive energy, signals from the universe, our intuition, our creativity, and our ability to manifest what we want in life.  But then, our "logic" overrides that blend and we quickly talk ourselves out of it.*

*I am asking, I am begging, and I am hoping that you will work on the inner courage and strength it takes to have a leap of faith in yourself and in any higher power that you feel connected with.  I am willing to support many extreme and unconventional ideas under certain conditions and special circumstances.*

*Life is not a one size fits all, cookie cutter type of experience. Allow these thoughts and ideas to flow and challenge yourself to take some risks. They will likely pay off for you in more ways than you expect. Good luck!*

*This is your mission, should you choose to accept it*

*25) Please consider a simple act of self care today, this week, and this weekend. Pick out something special you can say about yourself and take a moment to meditate on how you can nurture that part of you in a small but meaningful way.*

*We can lose ourselves easily. Try to recapture some things about yourself that you honor and appreciate. Imagine that you are worthy of at least a tad more joy in your life and that you will actively take small steps to achieve that. Visualize those positive attributes and notice how good that feels. Building upon that is not selfish or hurtful/frustrating to others. If people around you react to changes you are making, try to not take that personally, try to understand that change is tough for people. It can be scary and unknown, even change for the better.*

*Thank you for considering this and keeping it in your mind and heart.*

*26) Often times when asked the question about something very special, something very magical, or something very powerful that a person would want to have or experience in their lives right now (not material things), people tend to pull away quickly from it. Rather than think too much about if that can happen, how realistic is it, if you are deserving, etc, allow it to marinate a bit. Enjoy the idea and try not to think too much about it. Rather, experience it in your mind, heart, and body as if it is in front of you right now. Sometimes that can help set the stage and prepare you for upcoming decisions that you will have to make, even ones that you are unaware will be in front of you.*

*Do not rule anything out that would offer you some joy, excitement, and rejuvenation. If it does not come to fruition, at least it was a pleasant thought and a healthy distraction from moment to moment stressors. And, you never know, maybe manifesting energy will work for you in ways you least expect and in the timing that you least expect or need it most.*

*27) Feeling stuck in frustration, anger, hurt? Here is quite an extreme challenge to help free yourself from circumstances beyond your control. It is a simple concept, not easy to do, and it is likely you will think that it will not "work."*

*I suggest an extreme act of vulnerability, share with whomever you consider to be your very best friend (soul mate) this dark place that you are in. Share the frustration, the anger, the hurt, how unfair it is, and the desire to release it. Speak this truth in a raw and honest way, in a way that you never have shared before. If you are not tearful during this exercise, you may not be doing it right. Dig down deep and share something that you cannot bare to say out loud, something that is tough for you to even think about.*

*Try this with that special person you keep very close to your heart. They will not have the answers, they will only be able to love, hug, comfort, and reassure. Ironically, that is not the thing that is most helpful in this exercise. The most helpful thing that will allow you to feel a release, and to free yourself from that invisible prison, is your act of vulnerability.*

*Holding things in for too long contributes to your feelings of sadness, depression, isolation, and hopelessness. This will help you with the beginning steps toward healing. You will then soon be able to focus and to work on strategies and solutions using your intellect, your heart, your intuition, and your spirit.*

*28) Are you an instrument of peace today? Not an easy question to answer. It may be in your heart, but strive for it to come out of you in every way that it can. Miscommunication is in the air in a strong way right now. Slow down, take time to think about what you are saying and what you are responding to with others.*

*Being an instrument of peace does not mean that you keep quite, let things go, or allow others to treat you poorly. It means that what you communicate and the way in which you communicate has a pure goal of achieving peace and harmony. That can be for as an inner goal, an outer goal, or to influence another by bringing something to their awareness in a way that is not attacking or destructive to them.*

*Try very hard to make decisions based upon what will enhance you and the ones you hold very close to your heart. If it does not serve you and your loved ones well, then perhaps you can let it pass until another time in which it does serve.*

*29) Negativity is extremely powerful and flowing all around us, it is not easy to do this but the idea is easy-we need to make an active and mindful decision every day and every hour to stay in positivity and light. That is hard to do when there is darkness around us, however, you are a peaceful warrior in this task. Move forward with conviction about yourself, your goals, your energy, and taking a proactive approach to positivity. Do not wait for it to happen!*

*30) Tears are special, they are a different type of water mixture within our body. There are people who have tears that flow often and people who rarely shed a tear. Either way, treat your tears as special and allow yourself to feel them as meaningful. Next time a tear "escapes" from your eye, try not to push it back in or wipe it away. Try allowing it to find its own path down your cheek and to the bottom on your chin. Let it dry there and pay attention to the sensation of that release. We often seem too much in a hurry to make them go away or to prevent them from coming out. Change that one time and see what happens.*

*31) Do you feel cherished by those who love you?*

*The word "cherished" is very important right now because it implies tenderness, gratitude, love, and viewing you in a much stronger way beyond your flaws and faults. If you feel cherished, you will feel love always and will be able to endure conflict, hurt, and frustration. At your core, you will at least know that the distress you feel is temporary instead of experiencing it as a prison sentence of darkness and solitude.*

*Here is the key to this concept, you will have to communicate your need to feel cherished by those who love you. Sometimes, we teach people how to treat us in a negative way. Change this and raise your standards of what you will tolerate and how you expect your loved ones or partner to treat you. In fact, demand it. However, remember that YOU will have to operate in this compassion as well. YOU will have to set the stage and provide an example of how to make your loved one feel cherished.*

*Close your eyes and allow yourself to drift to a peaceful, calm, and warm place deep within yourself. Pay attention to your breathing and relaxing your muscles. Then visualize what it would look like to be cherished. Hear an inner voice whispering in your ear that you want, need, and deserve to be cherished. As you open your eyes, continue to visualize the word "cherished" and speak in ways that create the space for you to feel that from your loved one.*

*Expect nothing less from now on!!!!!*

*32) There are people that touch us in small but significant ways. They enter our lives, sometimes for only a moment, but the profound effect they have can be lasting. If this reminds you of anyone you know that you keep close to your heart, then send them a quick message that tells them how much they mean/meant to you and that your heart is warmed whenever you think of them.*

*This will offer two things, the first that you will broadcast positive energy and that frequency will help bring this energy back to you. And, the second, that it will offer them a touching moment followed by a nice smile. They will not be able to contain a brief feeling of joy that they matter and that someone appreciates them and finds them to be valuable.*

*Try to think of two or three people that you would put in this category and reach out to them, even if it is just in a sentence or two.*

*To some who read this, you fall into that category for me and I want you to know that I keep you in my thoughts and close to my heart. Thank you!*

*33) Is your soul on empty? Are you searching for something?*

*You can find what you are looking for deep within. You can replenish yourself and manifest the abundance of what you need in love, support, and guidance. Clear your mind from the constraints and parameters that hold you down and that stand in your way. Try to not "think" about what you are looking for, let it be revealed to you, ask and pray for the clarity and wisdom that you seek to fulfill what you need.*

*If you are finding reasons why you cannot get what you need, then you are blocking yourself before you have even begun. Drop the pebble into the pond, so to speak, and see where the water ripples out. Let that be your guide as you explore a new world in front of you, one that you get to take more ownership of.*

*34) Do you have the courage to take some risks today? How about in two ways? The first one being to take a risk by sharing an act of compassion with someone who you feel distant from or perhaps even hurt by. This is a big challenge because you may not feel that they deserve it, but think of it this way.... There is so much pain, negativity, and hurt right now, that it could do you some good to simply say/acknowledge something small that meant something to you. Even something a small as a partner pouring you a cup of coffee. Transform your energy deep within by allowing yourself to say something of gratitude and meaning, even if only for a moment. It will help you in the long run.*

*The second challenge would be to take a risk of upsetting someone you care about by saying "no, I'm sorry but that is too much for me right now." Even if you want so much to love and care for that person, setting a boundary right now is critical for several reasons. The first is self care and practicing what it is like to make decisions that work best for you first, then for others. The second is that there is so much energy drain right now, it is important to conserve as much energy as possible before the holidays approach. And third, people need to see and learn from healthy examples of self care and setting boundaries.*

*If for some reason, people get upset with you for slowing your output down a tad, then use that as an opportunity to educate them in these notions of self care and goals of peace and balance. They may not understand or agree but it is critical that they be given an opportunity to hear what your intention is and that it is not an act against them.*

*Good luck!!!!*


*35) What comes first, self-confidence or faith in yourself?*

*If you have confidence in yourself, having faith in yourself will follow. However, having faith in yourself and acting on it will lead to self-confidence.*

*Perhaps it starts with having faith in yourself because this requires an active choice, a decision to believe that there is something inside of you that is competent and that will lead you in the right direction. Self-confidence usually comes from experiencing successes in the outcome of your abilities.*

*People often mention that it is important to have self-confidence. That is true, however, there can often be a whisper of a negative inner voice saying something like "yeah, that's nice and all, but this probably won't work and I'll mess it up in some way." We can often talk ourselves out of self-confidence and talk ourselves into self-doubt.*

*However, choosing to have faith in yourself allows you to continue a positive momentum that is independent from any outcome. It is like saying, "I believe that I have abilities and qualities that can help me and I'm going to operate on the principle of faith; a belief that things CAN work for me and that I CAN make good decisions." For now, that is all that we need to start with. Having self-confidence is great, however, there is a loop-hole in that we can talk ourselves out of it.*

*Conversely, having faith allows for much more vague grounding, it is hard to argue with vague and ambiguous concepts. This is probably a good way to safe-guard self doubt. It is much harder to argue against something that remains open and faith based.*

*Try this one time and share with people about the shift you will feel being in a little more control of your inner state of being.*


*36) Let us all try to raise our collective consciousness to create more peace, stability, and balance around us. We are all noticing that no one is immune to distress and chaos right now. The solution can only be through a joint effort. At the end of 2012, some were preparing for the apocalypse and end of times. 2013 was a transitional year, a time of extreme difficulty for many. Let us please try to change the energy for the rest of 2014, a year that should be restorative and healing to us all.*

*This is a task assigned to all of us, please start to do this in your own way, internally and externally. We need each other and a new found hope that things will get better!*

*37) When the struggle is too much to bear, we are often left feeling broken, hopeless, and questioning what we have done to deserve this "punishment." Though I cannot offer a phrase to make things "seem" better, I can suggest that the goal in those trying and dark moments can be to simply hold on, to endure, and to outlast. We tend to act in desperation and impulse, sometimes taking necessary action, but sometimes operating in forced energy rather than in stillness.*

*It can be important to stay as present as possible moment by moment, sometimes avoiding our philosophical urge to catastrophize our situation. We can make things worse by inferring the meaning of the situation based on what it "feels like."*

*Try to not allow your thoughts to take over and thus contribute to complication and upset. Instead, try to think of these moments as challenges to stay present, grounded, and as a task oriented as possible.*

*There is a lot of struggle right now, it is hard to make sense of it and to try to track its origins or purpose. It is okay to just focus on maintaining as much sanity and self control as possible in the midst of the storm. Slow things down and keep moving forward inch by inch.*

*38) Even through extreme tragedy, upset, disappointment, and pain, there can also be powerful moments that allow for healing and peace within the heart. Try to allow your soul to drift towards those moments, recognizing them or creating them. Sometimes in the process of acceptance and management of something negative, we can find new ways of thinking and feeling that offer us a way to reconcile that pain and negativity; a way to disarm the effect it has on us. It is like acquiring a new skill that you could not have gained without enduring the stress.*

*I am not sure that I would go as far to say that something good always comes out of something negative, or that there is always a reason for something negative. More so, I would say that it is our task to endure and to manage the negative, the thing that is out of our control. That process can be cathartic and empowering.*

*Please try to keep that in mind when it feels like you are backed into a corner, pushed down, and stuck in a deep and dark place. There is light and love around you, it is available from deep within and externally if you are open to it and allow it. Challenge yourself by setting the intention to really sit with upset feelings, process what they mean to you, how you understand them and how you want to respond. Our tendency may be to avoid or to retreat or to numb, but instead, be mindful about experiencing. It will be difficult and taxing, but mastery of this will allow for so much more confidence and control.*

*39) There are new beginnings in the works around us. They may seem scary and overwhelming but try to have faith that things are moving in positive directions. If it is challenging and anxiety provoking, causing us some fear and doubt, there is a good possibility that it is something worth while for us to pursue. Think about some important decisions made in life: a school to attend, a car or house to purchase, a job, a relationship, marriage, or having a family. These are all things that can become overwhelming and stressful regardless of whether or not they are welcomed and exciting changes.*

*Maybe the shifts that are occurring around us are cues that it is time to make some changes? Perhaps there are opportunities worth pursuing that may cause more anxiety initially but that may ultimately offer more peace and balance. If you are reading this, then it is likely that this message is applicable to you. Whether you stumbled across this page, if it was shared with you or recommended to you, the message here today is based on an observation and sense that you need some encouragement to seek these challenges in front of you, to face them head on, and to prevail with a feeling of empowerment and victory.*

*Fear based reactions are completely unacceptable because they completely minimize your ability to manage, cope, and to make good intuitive based decisions. There are valid things that trigger fear for us; the unknown, finances, risks, failure, pressure, people's reactions, life changes, schedule, etc. However, try to not let those small whispers in your ear become loud paralyzing sounds. Allowing fear to block your positive shift will lead to suffocating your spirit and will contribute to continued old and negative patterns (namely, darkness).*

*Let us work on shedding these older ways of thinking, feeling, and behaving. Let us have faith that there is support and guidance out there for us from sources that we cannot always see, expect, or feel. It exists none the less, just like the internet. Where is the internet? How do we know it exists? Because we tap into it, we log in, we use it to access other things. We even used to pay per hour on dial-up to get there. Go in peace and strength today and everyday from now on!*

*40) Open your heart and mind. Prepare to receive love. Try to focus energy into your loved ones, gently and subtly whispering in their ears that you need that love in return. It is important to keep love and warmth flowing right now, much like it is important to stretch muscles before and after exercise.*

*As the weather changes, the sun shines, and things blossom, the same holds true for our mind, body, and soul. Reawaken from the hibernation of the winter and prepare for soulful movement.*

*Please do not limit yourself or short change yourself right now. Keep things flowing in a positive and simple direction. It is very easy to be derailed by stress, anxiety, and fear. One way to protect the self during moments like this is through active and mindful presence. Be vigilant about staying in the moment and not getting ahead of oneself.*

*Read and hear this with all of your senses and allow nature to nurture you right now.*

*41) Have you ever wondered why it seems easier to feel upset or angry? It does appear to be much easier to operate in darkness and to get stuck in raw emotion. Perhaps because it is not worth it or valuable to linger in these emotions?*

*Acquiring something worth having requires effort, like peace and happiness for example. They are easy choices for us, but not easy paths to pursue. It takes vigilance and the strategic application of persistence. Keep at it; it is worth it.*

*42) If you are struggling right now and cannot seem to figure out how to pull yourself out of a rut, there is a strong chance that you may need a hug. Please do not be afraid to ask for one from those whom you love and care for. Though the hug may not solve the problem or nature of the stress, research does show that it helps on a physiological level by changing chemistry within the body and brain. Plus, it feels really good to get a hug and to experience the love and intention in which it was given.*

*When you do hug, make sure that it is about 20 seconds long and has a firm enough of a embrace that lets you "feel" supported. A simple pat on the back will not suffice.*

*43) Please read this and hear the words whisper in your heart and soul. There is little room for self doubt and low confidence. If you can really dig deep and find your true identity, you can feel proud about who you are and the unique way that you live life. Share it with others and feel worthy of having a place on this earth. You are here for a reason and "we" need you. But we "need" the true "you!" Not the you that is influenced by fear, doubt, and negativity.*

*There are times in which you shine because, when you are not thinking too hard about it, you do things that that are amazing in the special way that you do them. Please work hard to trust yourself and to listen to the inner voice that knows truth and reality.*

*Sometimes people feel stuck in hurt/despair, relationships, work/career, and much much more. The way to release yourself from that inner prison is to tap into the purity deep within and to feel the divine creation of your existence. You owe it to your spirit to honor and cherish yourself and to find the things that nurture you and foster your growth and flourishing.*